Mr. Everit's

Secret

Also by Alan H. Cohen

BOOKS

Are You as Happy as Your Dog?
Dare to Be Yourself
A Deep Breath of Life
The Dragon Doesn't Live Here Anymore
Handle With Prayer
Happily Even After
Have You Hugged a Monster Today?
I Had It All the Time
Joy Is My Compass
Lifestyles of the Rich in Spirit
Looking in for Number One
My Father's Voice
The Peace That You Seek
Rising in Love
Setting the Seen
Why Your Life Sucks (and What You Can Do About It)
Wisdom of the Heart

CASSETTES/CDs

Deep Relaxation
Journey to the Center of the Heart
Living from the Heart
Peace

VIDEO

Wisdom of the Spirit

Alan H. Cohen

Mr. Everit's
Secret

What I Learned
from the World's
Richest Man

HAMPTON ROADS
PUBLISHING COMPANY, INC.

Hampton Roads Publishing Company, Inc.
1125 Stoney Ridge Road
Charlottesville, VA 22902

434-296-2772
fax: 434-296-5096
e-mail: hrpc@hrpub.com
www.hrpub.com

If you are unable to order this book from your local
bookseller, you may order directly from the publisher.
Call 1-800-766-8009, toll-free.

Library of Congress Cataloging-in-Publication Data

Cohen, Alan, 1950-
  Mr. Everit's secret : what I learned from the world's richest man /
Alan H. Cohen.
       p. cm.
ISBN 1-57174-416-9 (alk. paper)
1. Success in business. I. Title.
HF5386.C726 2004
650.1--dc22
                                                          2004004397
           10 9 8 7 6 5 4 3 2 1

Printed on acid-free paper in the United States

To Dr. William Cleghorn,

who reminded me that well-being is natural.

Table of Contents

Introduction

Life has an amazing way of sending help to those who need it. For many years I have worked intimately and intensively with people who have faced and moved beyond difficult and sometimes overwhelming challenges. I have heard one common theme from nearly all of them: *When I most needed help, it showed up. Life did not leave me to drift and die. To the contrary, my ordeal led me to greater life.*

The story you are about to read is a chronicle of the answer to one such man's prayers. Although he would not call himself a spiritual man, and certainly not a religious one, his heart was in deep pain and his spirit called out for relief. His answer showed up in the form of Bert Everit.

Although the story is couched in an apparently fictional format, I assure you that the lessons recounted in *Mr. Everit's Secret* are quite real. They occurred during real life on planet earth to people like you and me. Somewhere in our world walks the man depicted as Bert Everit in the pages that follow. Although you may not recognize him, you do know him. And he knows you. He has already found you, or he will. Of this you can be sure.

The man himself, he asked me to tell you, is less

important than the lessons he delivers. Mr. Everit is not interested in fame, accolades, or personal attention. Please, he urges you, do not confuse the medium with the message. Teachers of truth come and go, and with them their human foibles. Yet the principles they impart are eternal and immutable, more solid than steel. They work because they are universal law. Mr. Everit sees himself simply as a voice for wisdom we all have, but need reminders to live. Thus he chooses to work quietly, out of the public eye.

Everything you need to know to achieve personal, financial, career, and relationship success is contained between these covers. Such a claim is not exaggerated; indeed to proclaim less would be to understate what is available here. If you latch onto even one of Mr. Everit's lessons, practice it, and make it real in your life, you are well on your way to mastering them all. "The truth is like a diamond," he once told me. "If you take any one facet and follow it all the way in, it will lead you to every other facet."

Enjoy your journey with Mr. Everit. He will make you think, laugh, and cry. Along the way he will hold up a mirror to your true face and shine a torchlight for your steps. Then he will creep into your heart like a long-lost friend you had forgotten how much you missed until you reunited with him. Then you will discover that, like Mr. Everit, the answer to your quest is closer to home than you know.

Alan H. Cohen

Mr. Everit's

Secret

The Great Wheelbarrow Caper

A laborer in a hardware factory went to the CEO and asked for a promotion. After a brief discussion, the CEO bluntly informed the man that he didn't have the education, experience, or business savvy to be a manager.

"Then I'll make you a wager," the laborer offered. "I say I am smart enough to make it look as if I am bringing the company business, but meanwhile rob the company blind without you knowing how. If I can pull this off, I'll return the goods and you give me the promotion. If not, I'll quit."

The CEO, being a sporting fellow, accepted the bet.

The next day at 5 P.M. the laborer showed up at the checkout of the factory store, pushing a wheelbarrow full of inexpensive items for his purchase. One by one, the clerk rang up each article. The laborer paid for all the products and took them home.

The next day the fellow showed up again at the company store with a wheelbarrow containing low-cost goods, and paid for them. And the next day, and the next.

The CEO, especially watchful for the laborer's deception, gave strict instructions to the store clerk to be sure that every item in the wheelbarrow was checked and paid for. He further ordered that the laborer be searched for concealed articles. None were found.

After a month, the company records showed a loss in profits. The next month revealed an even greater drop. By the end of the quarter, the company was in the red and no one could figure out why.

Finally the CEO called the laborer into his office and conceded the bet. "Now you must tell me what you have been stealing," he demanded.

A sneaky grin grew on the laborer's face as he answered, "Wheelbarrows."

Stars Beyond the Telescope

Some people say that before we are born we make a date to meet everyone in our life who will affect our destiny. If I knew how much one odd man would change my world, I would have found my way to him when I was younger. But, then again, he taught me that there's a timing to life. Still, there are so many things I wish I had said to him. Maybe if I tell you my story, he will somehow hear. . . .

I showed up for my interview at the wheelbarrow factory twenty minutes late. Bert Everit emerged from his little office wearing a new pair of Wranglers and a plaid flannel shirt just big enough to contain his modest Buddha belly. He greeted me warmly and shook my hand for a long time. I worried for a moment that he was going to hug me, but he didn't.

"I've been waiting for you," he told me right off.

Had I blown the job before I even got hired? I couldn't afford that; my credit report was getting uglier by the day. "Sorry I'm late . . . There was traffic on—"

"No, no, don't worry about that," he laughed. "I was just looking forward to meeting you."

Did this guy greet every job applicant like this? Before I could make sense of his welcome, he whisked me off and introduced me to all the department heads as if I was a long-lost family member. Along the way he rested a comforting hand on my shoulder, looked me squarely in the eye, and asked me more questions about my life than my skills. In the hour I spent with him, he gave me more undivided attention than my therapist.

I wasn't surprised when Mr. Everit invited me to stay for dinner. He escorted me to his studio apartment at the back of the factory, an oddball Hobbit hut strewn with a turtle shell from the Galapagos, overdue Anthony Robbins videos, and a rare collection of Yoda action figures. I had met people like him before. They were either nuts or geniuses. Maybe both.

He donned a chef's hat personally autographed by Wolfgang Puck, cooked us up a tasty Cajun halibut, and then unlocked his private stash of cognac. I was astounded to watch this strange duck move with disarming simplicity, a homespun blend of mastery and humility.

After dinner he took me out on his little patio overlooking a lush valley, where I could hear critters rustling in the night. "How good is this?" he uttered with eyes aglow as he inhaled a deep breath of country air. The moon had not yet risen, and in the dark of the night sky I was awestruck by a shimmering splash of stars across the heavens.

"Can you believe all those stars?" I asked him.

"I can believe them—that's why I see them," he answered. "Dominic didn't skimp on anything."

Dominic? I turned to him and squinted, "Who the heck is Dominic?"

"Dominic is my name for God."

"Then why don't you just say, 'God?'"

"The word's gotten too beat up over the years. I like 'Dominic.'"

Okay, Dominic it is.

"Dominic created the universe in fantastic abundance. Extravagant, even. Niagara Falls was His idea—not those silly little contraptions you put on your shower to save water. Jeez, you have to stand there twice as long to get wet. So what's the point? Ecologists should take a hint."

I just sat there taking it all in, wondering if Bert Everit was an incognito sage or one fry short of a Happy Meal.

"Right where you're looking now, there are millions of stars," he went on, losing himself in a gaze. "And billions more beyond them." He clasped his hands behind his head and leaned back so far I was afraid he would fall over. "You could build a telescope bigger than Mt. Everest, and there would still be countless stars past its range. The universe is a bean counter's nightmare, but a mystic's delight."

I never really thought of the universe as endlessly rich. I spent more time trying to figure out how to time my coming and going from my apartment so my landlord wouldn't corner me.

"Have you ever been to Hawaii?" he asked abruptly.

Hawaii? Are you kidding? "Only seen it on TV and the movies."

"I went there on my honeymoon with Marlene. It's quite a place. Everything is gigantic! Palm leaves so big it takes two guys to load one in a truck. I asked a couple who live there, 'Do you have seasons in Hawaii?' The lady snickered, 'Yes—every fall we argue over who is going to rake the leaf!'"

Was that really true, or was he just making this up as he went along?

"Ever been to Australia?"

"Nope."

"I was there on business once. Saw a statue of a 12-foot prehistoric kangaroo. Momma! Can you imagine driving around a corner and running into one of those suckers?" He slapped his thigh and laughed; he obviously got a kick out of himself.

"Ever been to prehistoric times?"

Did he, like, take me for a complete geek? "Uh . . . not that I remember."

"Once, in a museum, I saw a replica of a prehistoric armadillo the size of a Volkswagen Beetle."

Okay, already. "And your point?"

He had toyed with me long enough. "Life was intended to be *big* and *a lot*. Everything, everywhere, in infinite supply, capable of reproducing itself in immeasurable quantities forever. Enough of everything for everyone. Always."

Well, that might be, I thought, but then why do I have to go to the gas station to fill up my saggy left rear tire with air before I can drive anywhere? If I could afford a new tire, I would just buy one. Meanwhile, people are starving, trees are disappearing faster than Burger King sells Whoppers, and tap water tastes like transmission fluid. "So what happened, Mr. Everit?" I asked him up front. "If the universe is so abundant, why have good things gotten so scarce and why doesn't everybody have everything they want?"

He stood there silently for a while. Maybe I stumped him, I thought. Finally he turned to me and asked, "Do you need to get anywhere soon?"

"I guess not. No dates with Britney Spears tonight."

"Then let's take a ride." Mr. Everit grabbed his keys and motioned for me to follow him.

what I learned from Mr. Everit:

- what I see is what I believe.
- The universe was created in utter abundance—even extravagance.
- For every limit I can imagine, there is something beyond it.

other stuff he said:

- Almost the whole world is asleep. Everybody you know, everyone you see, everyone you talk to. only a few people are awake, and they live in constant total amazement.

  (From the film Joe Versus the Volcano)

- If all you're receiving for your work is money, you're being grossly underpaid.
- choose a job you love, and you'll never work another day in your life.

what I did

- used Mr. Everit's computer to look him up on the Internet to see if he had a criminal record or had been institutionalized.
- wondered if there is more available than I've been settling for.
- started to notice signs of enoughness in and around me.

Lesson 2

Pygmy Thoughts

We drove about ten minutes along an old country road dotted with speed limit signs pockmarked with bullet holes by local yahoos. Stupid people with guns seemed to poke a big hole in Mr. Everit's "life is good" theory. Yet as I watched the full moon rising over a rolling meadow, I felt a sense of peace. Living in the city for so long, I don't remember the last time I paid much attention to the moon. Was there life beyond the flashing time and temperature sign?

Without a word, Mr. Everit pulled his silver 4-Runner (he named it "Big Buck") off to the side of the road and parked next to a corral of weathered gray rough-cut logs. For a moment I grew leery; I hardly knew this dude, and here I was alone with him in the middle of nowhere. He was definitely a little quirky. What if he had a chainsaw in the back of his truck? Or if he was a terrorist, or a member of some weird cult that needed a full moon sacrifice? Or, or, or . . . ? My mind spun out for a while, but reason reassured me my fears were unfounded. Eccentric as he was, he seemed very kind; if I was safe with anyone, it was him.

Bert Everit stepped out of Big Buck with a John Wayne-like half poise, ambled to the corral fence, and leaned over it. I took the hint and followed. Suddenly I heard the stirring of hooves in the pasture; within a few moments several tiny horses approached us. They were so small that at first, in the ambiguous moonlight, I thought they were large dogs, about the size of a big German Shepherd. As they came closer, I could see they were horses for sure.

"Are those Shetland Ponies?" I asked.

"Nope. They're Pygmy Horses."

I'd never seen such strange creatures before. "How do they get so small?"

"Breeding," he replied with a forced little smile. "Way back when, someone mated the two smallest horses they could find. Then they took the offspring and bred them with the other smallest horses they could find. And on and on, like that. Every generation, the horses got smaller and smaller, until they ended up the tiny specimens you see before you."

"That's amazing!"

"Yes, isn't it? When you put two small things together, the results get only smaller."

Mr. Everit deftly boosted himself onto the fence and sat facing the Pygmy Horses. Again I followed. My move, however, was clumsier. I nearly fell over into the corral, until he caught me and steadied me. I felt like a dweeb.

Finally I got settled, and we sat in the stillness for a while. I figured that him bringing me here was his way of fielding my question. "What does this have to do with how things got scarce in our world?" I asked him.

"Everything," he answered, straightening his John

Deere cap. "Over many, many generations, people have cultivated pygmy thoughts. Not purposely, mind you—but that doesn't matter. Habits affect you whether you mean them or not. Every time you assume, 'there's not enough' or 'I'm not enough' and you get together with someone who agrees, you just bred a pygmy thought. You just made your world smaller."

As if on cue, a little dappled mare approached us. Mr. Everit leaned down and stroked her forehead. The moon shadows accented deep wrinkles at the side of his eyes, the kind that spoke of traveling many trails. "When millions of people keep thinking 'not enough' and fueling their belief with fear, the world shrinks daily."

I tried to shift my position on the fence. My butt hurt. Maybe I was uncomfortable with the subject.

"I don't know, Mr. Everit," I challenged him, "Do you really think everyone is that stupid?"

"I didn't say 'stupid,'" he answered soberly. "Just asleep . . . They don't realize they shape their destiny with every thought and word."

The mare ambled over to me and began to nuzzle my leg.

"Then what if some big thinker wrote a book or went on television or got elected President," I suggested, "and told people they could have a lot more than they've been settling for? You know, like the kid who shocked everyone into admitting that the Emperor wasn't wearing clothes . . .Wouldn't people figure out how to be rich if they didn't believe they had to be poor?"

Mr. Everit shook his head. "Only those ready to hear it. Most people feel safe in their familiar little world—even if it stinks. It's like that movie *The Truman Show*, where the guy grows up on a life-size TV set and thinks it's real. When he figures out the plot and struggles to escape, someone asks the show's producer if Truman can break free. The producer explains, 'He can get out anytime he wants. The truth is, he prefers his world.'"

I started to feel agitated. A few of the horses let out a whinny. The wind, which had been still, whipped up, and I began to feel a chill.

"Back in medieval times people believed the sun revolved around the earth," Mr. Everit went on. "When Galileo suggested that the earth revolved around the sun, the church prosecuted him for heresy and sentenced him to life imprisonment."

"I know, I know," I snapped. "Tenth grade science."

"Ignorance still rules," he shot back. "A hundred years from now, people will look back on a lot of stuff we do, and ask, '*What were they thinking, anyway?*'"

One of the horses nodded his head vigorously. My rear end was numb. Everit had a lot of nerve to imply that my financial predicament was my own doing.

"People cling to their little fishbowl lives and resist change like the plague," he insisted. "Meanwhile they are starving at a dinner in their honor."

"Okay, since you brought up starving, if life is so rich, why, with all our technology, do children still starve to death?"

"War, usually," he answered curtly. Then, like a magician, he pulled a small apple out of his pocket, broke it into pieces, and gently fed them to a few little horses.

"War?"

"During the war in Bangladesh, for example, people from all over the world sent boatloads of food to alleviate the famine. But fighting blocked the provisions from getting to the hungry people. The rations sat and rotted in the bellies of the boats at the dock . . . best-fed rats in the world. Dominic didn't create the shortage. People did."

"Oh, come on now!" I protested. "Plenty of people are hungry because they can't afford to eat."

"And what keeps money from circulating? Not Dominic. People. Take September 11th, for example. A bunch of idiots crashed airplanes into big buildings and killed thousands of people. That's tragic. The only thing sadder was what happened afterward. Millions of people got scared and shriveled up. Fear immobilized them, and for a long time they quit flying and spending money. Marlene's sister is an optometrist in Pennsylvania. She told me that for a year after September 11th, people stopped buying eyeglasses. Now if you can explain to me how a bunch of fanatic whackos in Afghanistan can keep little old ladies in Pennsylvania from buying spectacles. . . ."

"The economy got depressed. . . ."

"No!—*People* got depressed!" he nearly shouted. "That made the economy depress. The economy has no mind of its own. Your car doesn't drive itself anywhere. You drive it. People drive the economy. Osama bin Ladin and his cronies did not cause the recession. Frightened people did. On September 12 there was just as much money to go around as there was on September 10. People just stopped circulating it. Pygmy thoughts, fertilized by terror, bred rapidly overnight."

Mr. Everit looked me in the eye with almost frightening intensity and told me, "The cause of poverty is not scarcity. It is fear and small thinking."

After a moment he took a long deep breath, relaxed, and asked, "Ready to head back now?"

"Okay," I answered. But I wasn't okay. Bert Everit was beginning to rock my world.

What I learned from Mr. Everit:

- I shrink my world when I think and talk small. It gets even smaller when people agree with me.
- People find strange comfort in living tiny lives, and resist change even if it might help them.
- The cause of poverty is not lack, but fear and withholding.

Other stuff he said:

- Great thinkers have always received violent opposition from mediocre minds. (Einstein)
- Those who say it can't be done are usually interrupted by others doing it.
- It's not a small world, after all.

What I did:

- On my way into Denny's for a late-night snack, did not buy the newspaper with scary headlines.
- Sat at the diner and made a list of stuff I would do if I were not afraid.
- Kept my mouth shut when the waitress started to complain about the economy, weather, and politics.

Lesson 3

The Hungry Fisherman

That night I lay awake for a long time, thinking about those Pygmy Horses. I had lots of people and conditions to blame for the things I lacked. A father who never came home; anal-retentive bosses; kamikaze terrorists; forked-tongued politicians; irrational women; a fickle stock market; hypocritical religion; greedy gasoline gougers; refineries that turned the air yellow; sexual- and computer-transmitted viruses; idiots who drive like they got their license at K-Mart; and on and on. In therapy I had traced my pain back to an overbearing mother angry at having to raise me by herself. An astrologer told me that money would always be a problem for me, and a psychic explained that I had been a debtor in a past life and I was still trying to undo that karma. My list of ways life had beaten me down was longer than Rush Limbaugh's criticisms of Democrats, and a lot more people would have sympathy for my problems than his. But if there was any truth to what Mr. Everit was saying, those people and things didn't really have power over me. And if that was so, how could I get my power back?

The next afternoon I drove back to the factory, where I found Mr. Everit in his apartment popping Goobers and watching a "Leave It to Beaver" rerun. He claimed that a few minutes of good belly laughs in the middle of the day freed his mind to figure out stuff he couldn't solve in the thick of work. I sat down and watched the second half of the show with him; I have to admit that by end of the program my financial situation didn't feel so impossible.

"What brings you back here?" he asked as he flicked off the TV.

"Well, first off, I was wondering if I got the job."

"Do you want the job?"

He obviously had no idea how much I *needed* the job. "Yes, I do."

"Then you have the job."

Cool. "But don't you have to run it by a committee, or board, or something?"

He laughed. "I *am* the board. If I like you, you're in . . . I like you. You're in." He shook my hand and then studied my face for a long moment, as if he was reading my mind. "There's more, isn't there?"

There was. "I've been pretty confused about what you told me last night," I confessed.

"Good."

"Good? What's so good about being confused?"

He stood up, walked toward his little refrigerator, and took out a bag of ground coffee. "Confusion is the last stop on the train to clarity," he told me. "The part of your mind that thinks it knows how it all is, is butting up against a bigger idea. It's only a matter of time until the smaller thought gives way to the greater. Don't fight it. Just try to enjoy the ride."

Did he really know all this stuff, or was he just a smooth talker?

"If I'm headed for such a good place, why do I still owe $27,421.57 in credit card bills?"

Mr. Everit sauntered to his Mr. Coffee machine and dripped some Kona Gold chocolate macadamia brew into an old maroon 49ers mug so chipped and cracked it should have been in a museum. Then he turned and ordered me, "Drive home now."

Oh, come on. "Did I finally stump you?" I blurted out. "Are you trying to get rid of me?"

"Drive home now by way of the Rosemont Street Bridge," he insisted, stirring his brew. "Do you know where that is?"

"Of course—it's a rickety old wooden bridge on the west side of town. It goes over a big stream just before you get out to Fairview."

"Do you have a cell phone?"

"Sure."

"Drive over the bridge and call me when you need to." With that, Mr. Everit put on his green and yellow cap and walked out the door to the factory floor. He didn't even say goodbye.

I just stood there, scratching my head. Was this man a Zen master, or a blue-ribbon fruitcake? I figured I'd give him one more chance.

I got in my car and drove twenty minutes to the bridge. There was no traffic, so I slowed way down as I approached. I had crossed this span hundreds of times and never noticed anything unusual. Had Mr. Everit created some bizarre scavenger hunt and posted some cosmic clue on one of the bridge's beams?

I drove across the bridge as slowly as possible and saw only a guy fishing at the foot of the bridge. People fish here all the time, I knew. I started to lean on the gas pedal, but something told me to stop. I pulled the car onto an embankment ten yards past the bridge and walked back. I stood at the railing and looked down at the fisherman.

Just then he caught a small trout maybe seven inches long, best I could see from above. He tossed the fish into a beat-up white plastic bucket and cast his line again. Five minutes later he reeled in another trout, considerably larger than the first. He studied the fish for a few moments, shook his head, and cast it back in the stream. Strange, I thought. I kept watching for about half an hour; during that time he caught several more fish. Oddly, the fisherman kept all the smaller trout and tossed the bigger ones back into the stream. It made no sense. Finally I decided to climb down the embankment to try and figure out what the fellow was up to.

"How's it goin'?" I asked him.

"Fair to middlin'" he answered in a monotone. "I come down here a couple times a week and fish for some dinner. I usually catch a bunch of trout and cook them up, but I'm still hungry. I'm doin' the best I can."

"Do you mind if I ask you a question?"

"Fire away, " he answered nonchalantly as he cast his line again.

"I've been watching you from the bridge for a while, and I notice that you keep the little fish and throw the big ones back into the stream. Why is that?"

"Simple," he answered. "I have this frying pan here that's about nine inches wide." Still holding his fishing rod with his right hand, the fisherman leaned over, picked up a small cast-iron skillet, and held it up so I could see. "Only the little fish fit in the pan, so those are the ones I keep."

I couldn't believe his reasoning. "Then why don't you . . ." I started to ask, but was interrupted by the short blip of a police siren at the top of the bridge. I scurried up to find a cop parked behind my car.

"This your car, mister?" he asked in a cop voice.

"That's right, officer."

"You can't park here. You're blocking the shoulder. You're gonna need to move it, or else I'll have to give you a citation."

"Sure, no problem."

I got into the car and started for home. My strange interaction with the fisherman had rattled me. What a peculiar way to fish! I picked up my cell phone and dialed Mr. Everit.

"So you met the hungry fisherman," he answered.

"I sure did. What a weirdo! The guy was wasting his energy on small fish. He'd sure save himself a bunch of work and eat a lot better if he just got a bigger frying pan!"

"Absolutely correct. Yet he's no weirder than anyone else who's hungry for money or anything."

"What do you mean?"

"Remember you asked me why you don't have everything you want, and how to get more?"

"Yes?"

"Get a bigger frying pan."

"What on earth are you talking about?"

"The frying pan is your mind. The fish represent your income, or anything you want more of. If you want to increase what you receive, first make a place for it in your mind. Think bigger thoughts; paint grander dreams. You can go to a gold mine with a tiny wheelbarrow or a huge one, and you will come away with as much gold as your container will hold."

I began to feel irritated and nearly veered across the road into an oncoming car. "But what about supply and demand?" I shouted into my cell phone. "And economic indicators? And focus groups?"

Mr. Everit laughed. I thought I could hear "I Dream of Jeannie" in the background. "Do you think I built this huge successful factory by listening to what other people told me was available?" he asked me. "Most people measure their possibilities by other people's measly frying pans and think that's all they can have. Only those who ask for more can get more, and only those who know more is available, ask."

I pulled off to the side of the road. "So why doesn't the hungry fisherman get the hint from the bigger fish he catches? He's holding the more that is available right in his hand!"

"Ah," Mr. Everit answered. "There's one more key ingredient."

"What's that?"

"I can't tell you. Someone else has to show you."

Here we go again.

"Are you free Friday night?"

"Of course I'm free Friday night. My social life resembles the color puke."

"Then meet me downtown. There's a sidewalk café called *Manga!* on Baylor Street. Go there for dinner, and I'll join you for dessert."

"Don't you want to come for dinner?"

It was no use asking. Bert Everit had already hung up, leaving me with another riddle and my own little frying pan.

what I learned from Mr. Everit:

- Laughter opens the door to answers I can't force.
- Instead of limiting life to my beliefs, I need to expand my beliefs to allow for all that life has to offer.
- Successful people pay more attention to their own visions and goals than to the history or opinions of others.

Other stuff he said:

- Life is too important to be taken seriously.
- Confusion means you're on the verge of a breakthrough.
- If you always do what you've always done, you'll always get what you've always gotten.

What I did:

- Made a list of my beliefs about money. (Yuk! No wonder it runs from me like I have B.O.)
- Wrote down what I would do with money if I were not in debt. (Come to Papa . . .)
- Started to focus on role models of people who have money and enjoy it, rather than those who consistently struggle over it.

Lesson 4

Crooked Beans

I found *Manga!* easily enough. It was a vibrant bustling restaurant in a run-down district; the place stood out like a polished opal in a tarnished setting. A steady stream of street people sauntered by customers dining on the patio—a real study in contrasts. Why Mr. Everit dispatched me here, I had no idea. Yet, knowing him even the little I did, this funky escapade did not surprise me.

The hostess, an attractive redhead with a pierced eyebrow and a Bart Simpson tattoo on her ankle, showed me to an outdoor table. I edged closer to an outdoor space warmer to offset the early evening chill. Feeling self-conscious as the only single diner, I buried myself in the menu and tried to look sophisticated.

An overly upbeat waiter came and took my order. (Could anybody really be *that* happy?) As soon as Smiley headed for the kitchen, a ragged-looking woman with a saucer-eyed little boy approached me from the sidewalk. "Excuse me, mister, I don't mean to bother you," she pleaded, "but my baby and I haven't eaten all day. We're so hungry. Could you please help us out?"

I was tempted to dismiss her, but I remembered Mr. Everit's lesson about the abundant universe. Not wanting to fall prey to Pygmy thinking, I reached into my wallet, took out a $20 and $5 bill, and handed them to her.

Her eyes lit up and she clutched my hand almost desperately. "Thank you so much, sir. God bless you."

I smiled and nodded. She stuffed the bills in her frayed jeans pocket and whisked away down the street, child on her hip. I felt warmer. When my dinner arrived, it was tastier for the satisfaction I took in knowing the woman and her little boy were eating a decent meal.

Dinner was uneventful. I picked at my rainbow tortellini, all the while wondering what possessed Mr. Everit to send me here. I could overhear the diners near me, yuppie couples on a field trip to the other side of the tracks. Ironic, I thought as they casually tossed their Diner's Club cards onto the checkerboard tablecloths while just a few doors down, families with more kids than money lived on Bud Light and Fritos, and considered McDonald's a five-star outing.

As the waiter brought the dessert tray, Mr. Everit showed up. He had an uncanny knack for timing, which was especially amazing since he didn't wear a watch. He arrived with his wife, Marlene, an attractive woman in her mid-fifties, with a proper highlighted bob, distinctive Mayan jewelry, and strong but tasteful makeup. Her elegance complemented Bert's down-home flavor; I liked her immediately. "How was dinner?" he asked as the two sat down.

"Okay," I answered in a blasé tone. "Would you care for some dessert?"

"Bert's a founding father in the Holy Church of

Chocolate," Marlene proclaimed proudly. "And I'm a charter member."

As soon as we had chosen our desserts, the woman who had approached me earlier appeared again. She and her son still looked forlorn. "Sorry to bother you again, sir, but could you possibly help us out some more? We're still hungry."

"What did you do with the $25 I gave you for dinner?" I had to ask.

"Oh, I don't have that anymore," she shrugged her shoulders. "I bought some lottery tickets."

I couldn't believe my ears! Just as I was about to give her a piece of my mind, the restaurant manager dashed out and shooed her away. "I'm sorry, folks," he apologized. "We'll be sure no one disturbs you again."

"Can you believe that?" I asked Bert and Marlene indignantly.

"Oh, I certainly can," Mr. Everit answered. "That woman is a good teacher of Crooked Beans."

"Crooked Beans?"

"When beans grow up in a crooked line, it means the seeds were planted in a crooked line. Weird money dramas bespeak weird money beliefs. It's no accident who has money and who doesn't, or when you have money and when you don't."

There he was, getting in my face again. "But some people are born into poverty and stay stuck for a lifetime," I argued.

"And right next door lives someone born into the same conditions, who works his way out and becomes a Bill Cosby, Lee Iacocca, or Martin Luther King. What do you think is the difference?"

"Genes? . . . Luck? . . . Fate?"

Mr. Everit shook his head. "None of that. It's mindset . . . attitude . . . intention . . . desire . . . willingness.

To get more money, a lot of people will change their job, car, home, marriage, and even their body. . . ."

"Like my friend Anne Jamison," Marlene interjected. "She had a nose job, tummy tuck, and face lift, and she still couldn't get a job."

Bert continued his thought, ". . . yet most people are unwilling to change the one thing that could help them most: their mind. So they work harder instead of smarter, keep going in circles, and end up no better off than they began. They're like the guy who discovers he is losing change out of a hole in his pocket, so he goes out and gets a second job to replace the lost money. How much easier would it have been to just sew the pocket?"

I was distracted for a moment by a metal chair scraping against the concrete patio. As the couple next to us got up to leave, the man left a fifty-dollar tip. Their dinner couldn't have cost a hundred.

"If you have a good wealth mentality," Mr. Everit went on, "you will generate wealth wherever you go. Even if you lose money temporarily, your wealth mentality will attract it again. If you have a lack mentality, no matter how much you receive or what financial opportunities come your way, wealth will evade you or, if it comes, it won't last."

Just then Mr. Upbeat delivered our desserts. Bert had ordered a Black Forest chocolate cake with caramel fudge sauce, which he dove into with reverential abandon. Marlene faced a mud pie taller than Mini-Me. I sat there looking at my orange sherbet.

After a few bites, Marlene asked Bert, "Didn't you tell me that if all the money in the world was redistributed equally among everyone, within a short time it would be back in its original hands in its original proportions?"

"But that doesn't sound fair," I objected before Bert could respond. "The rich stay rich and the poor stay poor!"

"A perfect demonstration of mind into matter!" Mr. Everit nearly shouted, banging the table with his hand, so hard that our dishes shook. "Your mind is like a powerful electromagnet that attracts experiences according to your beliefs. Mirrors don't lie, and neither does your checkbook."

I dared not tell them how many times my checkbook has gotten so screwed up that I just closed the account and started a new one.

"No need to fret," he consoled me as if he knew I was on a first-name basis with my bank's customer service manager. "No one is locked into any state of mind or wealth forever. The same mind that built the prison can build a way out."

I peered down the street where the panhandling woman had gone. "Your attempt to help that woman was sincere," Mr. Everit complimented me, "but she did not know how to use the money wisely. You can't help someone who is not ready to be helped. She needed wisdom more than dollars."

Mr. Everit offered me a bite of his chocolate extravaganza. I hesitated at first, but then took a taste; it exploded on my tongue like gooey fireworks.

Marlene watched my reaction and shoveled a generous slice of mud pie onto my plate. Then she told me, "A high school friend of mine believed the government should help people in inner cities by giving them money to get their lives together. After graduation she volunteered for Vista. After working in a ghetto area for a year, she changed her tune. Every Friday she watched people cash their welfare checks and go right to the liquor store. She decided that what they needed was not money, but self-worth, education, and motivation to use their money for things that could really help them."

Mr. Everit reached over to an empty table where someone had left a copy of today's newspaper. The headline shouted, *State Lottery Jackpot Goes to $32 Million.* "Most people who win big state lotteries revert to their former level of wealth within five years," he noted. "Some go through their money in weeks or months. Some drink themselves to death, and others commit suicide. Meanwhile, other winners enjoy their money, thrive, and help others. So money is not the answer to problems; wealth mentality is. If you were happy before you made your fortune, you will be happy with it. If you were unhappy without money, more money will only make you more miserable. It's the attitude you bring to your money that makes the difference."

"Like, 'engage brain before checkbook'?"

Happy Waiterman placed the tab on the table, and Mr. Everit attempted to snatch it. Quickly I grabbed it back. "That's very kind of you," I told him, "but I had a whole dinner and you just had dessert."

"And you just shelled out $25 for lottery tickets that are sure to lose," Marlene noted.

"That's right," I came back, "but the lesson that woman taught me about wealth mentality was worth a lot more than $25."

"My, my," Bert Everit smiled, "your beans are getting straighter by the minute."

What I learned from Mr. Everit:

- My finances mirror my beliefs and expectations.
- Money is important, but a wealth mentality is essential.
- When I change my mind, my situation changes to reflect it.

Other stuff he said:

- You can get over being poor, but it takes longer to get over being ignorant.
- It's hard to defeat an enemy who has an outpost in your head.
- Your thoughts are the strongest currency at your disposal.

What I did:

- Considered my financial situation and asked myself, "What would someone have to believe in order for this to happen?"
- Quit blaming Henry Farber for not paying me back the $50 I loaned him. I didn't expect him to pay it back, and he proved me correct.
- Asked Henry Farber to pay me back. Now I know I deserve it, and he will prove me correct.

Lesson 5

Borrowed Photos

I didn't tell Mr. Everit—or anyone—that I never had my own office before. I'd been working in a tiny cubicle for so long that I felt like a cheap plastic prize in a square gray Crackerjack box. The thought of looking out a window and seeing something green was, for me, tantamount to Dorothy landing in the Land of Oz.

At the end of my third week at the factory, my car was in the shop for the hundred eighty-eleventh time in three years. My mechanic told me not to bother trying to sell it; just squeeze it as hard as you can, he suggested, add sugar, and open up a stand in front of your house. As usual, the car was not ready by the end of the day, so Mr. Everit offered me a ride home.

"Mind if we stop off at Costco on the way back?" he asked as we turned out of the factory driveway. "Marlene asked me to pick up some groceries."

Hmmm. "Good call," I replied. "I need to pick up some photos I left there to be developed."

As we entered the Costco parking lot we passed a tattered, dreadlocked guy about my age, leaning into a dumpster, pulling out dented cans of Spaghetti-O's and tossing them into his rusty shopping cart full of junk. I remembered Mr. Everit's crooked beans lesson; could this poor guy find his way out of hell by changing his thinking? I tried to picture him all cleaned up, wearing a fresh-pressed Armani suit, living on Sterling Place in an off-white gabled Cape Cod house with a silicone-breasted wife and soccer-playing children. But then again, I figured, people in that position have their own crooked beans to deal with. And I certainly had my own.

I found my way to the long bin of packets of processed photos, alphabetized for customer pickup. I began poring through the array of envelopes, but I couldn't find mine. I had dropped them off over a week ago. Could someone have stolen my high school reunion pictures? There was no way I could replace them, and I started to feel irked.

"Having trouble?" I heard a voice ask. I turned and saw Mr. Everit, holding a package of salmon and a large banana cream pie with chocolate sprinkles.

"I think someone stole my photos," I reported dryly.

"Highly unlikely," he deduced in a Sherlock Holmes tone. "Let's look in some other sections." He set down his groceries and we began to pick through the other letters. After a minute he called out, "Ah! Here they are—just misfiled." Mr. Everit triumphantly pulled out the packet and handed it to me. I breathed a sigh of relief and opened it. There were my cherished photos. Except I looked fat.

"No one steals photos from this bin," he noted authoritatively. "Do you know why?"

"The honor system?"

"Even simpler: No one wants to take someone else's pictures home. Would you really want to see

Joshua Bernstein shaking hands in his Bar Mitzvah reception line? Or little Ashleigh pounding her high chair, with goopy Gerber's carrots dripping off her chin? Or Clyde and Maude Henderson feeding nickels to a slot machine on their golden-ager vacation to Vegas?"

Well, that was a no-brainer.

He grew more serious. "Distasteful as that sounds, you've taken home thousands of other people's pictures that are a lot more horrid than those."

Ayeee. "What are you talking about? I've never stolen any photos."

"I'm not talking about these," he asserted, holding up a packet and shaking his head. "You've taken home other people's pictures of reality. We all have. You absorbed your parents' and teachers' fears and prejudices about money and everything else. It's no wonder you grew up struggling. Poverty, you see, is hereditary—unless you change your mind while you still can."

A chill of fear rippled through me. "You mean I was brainwashed at a young age?"

Mr. Everit fingered through my reunion pictures and firmly said, "Long before you met any of these people."

I could feel my gut contract. "So I can blame my mother and stepfather for my money problems?"

He shook his head. "Once you start blaming, there's no end. You can't go back and hang the first amoeba."

"Well, then, parents should watch what they say to their kids," I argued.

Mr. Everit strolled across the aisle, picked up a Sony digital camcorder on sale, and peered through the viewfinder. "It's less what your parents said about money, and more what they did," he replied, aiming the camera at me. "They taught you in ways far deeper than words."

"You mean, like, body language?"

"More than that. Let's say you asked your mother for some money for candy. She went to her purse, took out a dollar, and gave it to you. But *how* she gave it to you influenced you more than *that* she gave it to you. If Mother extracted the bill like a martyr and resentfully handed it to you with the unspoken inference, 'We have so little and you are bleeding me for more,' you absorbed that message far more deeply than the dollar."

Did this man know my mother? She responded to my requests for small change as if I was applying for a million-dollar mortgage; by the time I was seven I felt like I was committing a sin just for asking. "Is that why I feel guilty when I think about having nice stuff?"

"You weren't born guilty. You were born bold and playful. Then you forgot who you are and what you deserve. When you remember who you were before you learned to apologize for asking, you'll have everything you want."

As Mr. Everit and I made our way to the checkout, I started to feel depressed. Was there any hope for me to get my creditors off my back?

"It's like you know the story of my life," I told him as we set our goods on the conveyer belt. "My dad was killed in Vietnam before I had a chance to meet him. He was listed as missing in action, and never came home. While my mother waited, she worked hard to raise me herself. She lived in constant fear that we wouldn't have enough. Even after she remarried, she clipped coupons as if they were stock certificates, and kept people waiting in line at supermarket checkouts while she scrutinized her receipt to make sure she wasn't overcharged. I went to school every day with a baloney sandwich on Wonder Bread and I brushed my teeth with generic toothpaste. Every item in our refrigerator and bathroom came in a black and white box. Now if I buy something in a color box, I feel extravagant! Sometimes I wonder how differently my life would have turned out if my dad had just shown up on my front porch one afternoon. . . ."

Suddenly Mr. Everit's eyes clouded and he started to look sad. "Are you okay?" I asked.

He took a while to answer. "Yeah," he stated in a low tone. "You just reminded me of someone I knew who went through the same kind of childhood." Laboring to gather himself, he urged me, "Go on."

I felt awkward and hoped I wasn't being a downer. I figured my best move was to just carry on. "Do you think I could learn to have more, Mr. Everit? Can you ever teach an old dog new tricks?"

"You have no idea what an old dog you are," he quipped.

The clerk handed me my receipt for my pictures. I opened the package one more time to make sure they were my own.

What I learned from Mr. Everit:

- I inherited my beliefs about money from my parents and other authority figures.

- We teach and learn through feelings, energy, and example more than words.

- I do not have to stay stuck with the "lack" messages I received. I can reprogram my mind by focusing on prosperity images now.

Other stuff he said:

- The present moment is your point of power.

- Creative minds have been known to overcome the worst programming. (Anna Freud)

- Feeling guilty is punishing yourself before God doesn't.

What I did:

- Wrote down the messages my parents and teachers gave me about money. (No wonder they were poor!)

- Decided which ones I want to keep, and which ones I want to let go of.

- Replaced my boring generic toothpaste with a colorful one with a classy pump.

Good Lemonade

Judging by the size and décor of his office, you'd never know he was the plant manager. He didn't have any diplomas or plaques on his wall, only photos of his radiant Marlene, paunchy fishing buddies Drew and Nelson, and New York fast-lane nephew Jason. He had no children of his own; if you brought up the subject, he would change it. As soon as you stepped through his door, he would invite you to sit in this big brown overstuffed leather chair with a crack in it that resembled a profile of John Lennon. Then he would open the lid of a Chief Red Cloud cigar box on the edge of his desk and offer you all the KitKat bars you could grab. Going to Bert Everit's office was more like visiting grandpa's house than the company CEO.

Maybe that's why I went to him when the psycho lady showed up.

"Sorry to bother you," I offered as I craned my head inside his slightly open door.

He looked up, saw it was me, and smiled. "What can I do for you?"

"Well . . . there's this, uh, strange woman in the showroom."

"Won't be the first time . . . What does she want?"

"She wants us to fix a wheelbarrow she bought last year."

"So let's just fix it . . . What's the big deal?"

"The big deal is that she didn't buy it here . . . It's a Demarest."

"She wants us to fix a Demarest she says she bought here?"

"We can't get rid of her."

He took a deep breath. "Let's take a walk."

Bert Everit put down the invoice he was studying, donned his cap, and headed for the showroom. I followed quickly. I had never seen him get upset with a customer; this could be a first.

There, sitting on the showroom's gray Formica counter, like a big red Irish Setter on a vet's examining table, was the Demarest. Bill, the showroom manager, and his assistant, Jeff, sat on stools behind the cash register, snickering like feisty crows on a low tree branch. The lady had been haranguing them for twenty minutes about the poor workmanship of our wheelbarrows. Now the big crow had arrived, and they had ringside seats to the showdown.

Bert Everit walked slowly to the Demarest and, like a vet palpating the Setter's hind leg, began to examine it. He took hold of the broken wooden handle and wiggled it. It had obviously cracked under pressure. At the center of the wheelbarrow, in obvious view, was the Demarest insignia.

"Looks like the wood just gave way here," he commented dryly.

The woman shook the broken piece. "That's right! And for the money I paid for this, the handle should last more than six months!"

I stepped back and folded my arms. This was going to be rich.

Mr. Everit thought for a moment, quietly scratching his chin. Then he answered, "I agree. You deserve a wheelbarrow that works for a long time." He turned to the showroom manager and politely ordered him, "Bill, would you please replace this handle?"

Bill stood up ramrod straight, with a shock on his face as if someone had run a fireplace poker up his hind parts. "But—" he began to object.

Mr. Everit dove in before he had a chance to finish. "Let's send Mrs. . . ?"

"Mrs. Ryan," the lady dutifully answered. "Dorothy Ryan, 5712 Charles Street."

"Let's send Mrs. Ryan home with a smile on her face." It was already there.

Mr. Everit shook the hand of Dorothy Ryan, 5712 Charles Street, bid her a good day, opened the door to the hallway, and nimbly walked through it like the ghost ballplayers in *Field of Dreams*. Quickly I followed.

"But Mr. Everit," I implored as soon as we were out of earshot of the showroom. "That wasn't even our wheelbarrow! Why would you go ahead and fix it?"

"Simple," he answered over his shoulder, hardly looking back. "She'll buy her next wheelbarrow here."

I followed him back to his office and just stood in the doorway, utterly befuddled.

"Sit down," he motioned toward the big brown leather chair. I consented, squashing John Lennon before he could object. As soon as I got settled, Bert told me, "You should read the company manual."

"I certainly did," I argued. "And it doesn't say anything about fixing another manufacturer's wheelbarrow."

"I'm not talking about *that* manual," he came back. "We have an advanced manual, simplified so anyone can master it." Then he ambled toward a small round glass table next to my chair and picked up a small book. It was the only one in his office. He handed it to me and told me, "This will answer more questions than I can."

I read the cover. It was a children's story called *Good Lemonade* by Frank Asch. I sat back and looked through the book. It was about a kid named Hank who decided to open a lemonade stand. On his first day, Hank sold a lot of lemonade. But then no one came back. So Hank mounted a massive marketing campaign. He painted the cups, offered discount deals, and hired go-go girls to dress up as lemons. Still, nobody bought Hank's lemonade twice. Then another kid opened up a lemonade stand down the street, and every day a long line of kids waited to buy his lemonade. Hoping to learn the other kid's secret, Hank stood in line to try his lemonade. When he tasted it, he realized it was really *good lemonade*. So Hank went home and mixed some more lemons and sugar into his formula. The next day there was a long line of kids at Hank's stand.

I closed *Good Lemonade* and set it back on the table. "You run your business on this book?"

"It reminds me that taking care of people is more important than getting something from them." He smiled and added, "Then the money comes, too."

I smirked and answered, "I could have used this book at the last two places I worked. Their manual was *Cheap Lemonade*. The company didn't care if anyone came back twice. They figured that if you got someone to buy something, you had succeeded—even if the thing fell apart when the customer got home. They spent a lot more money on advertising than customer care. The whole time I worked for them, I felt like a sleazy used car salesman who knew the odometers were turned back."

"And the reason you're not working there now is . . . ?"

"They went belly up."

"I see," he returned with his *Columbo* nod. Sometimes when he spoke the least, he said the most. "Feel like going for a ride?"

He had to be kidding. "Where to?"

"To look at some cars."

"Look at cars? In the middle of the day? . . . What about the Ace spreadsheet?"

"Oh, come on, live a little, would you?" he chided me. "The purpose of life is not to arrive safely at death."

We drove downtown to a Ford dealership, where Mr. Everit began to poke around some trucks on the lot. Soon a hungry salesman hurried out to meet us. "That engine's actually made by Mazda in Japan," he called to us from a distance. "How ya doin'? My name's Carl . . ."

Strange, I thought, that the salesman's first selling point was that the car's engine was manufactured elsewhere. As we began to follow Carl around the lot, I asked Mr. Everit why the guy would be so eager to point that out.

"You can thank W. Edwards Deming for that."

"W. Edwards *who*?"

"Back in the 1950s, Deming was an industrial quality guru who tried to convince Detroit automakers that they would be smarter to produce cars better and safer at the factory rather than fix them later. But his words fell on deaf ears. So Deming took his ideas to the Japanese, who were impressed with his concepts and put them into action. Pretty soon American consumers discovered that Japanese cars worked better, and they started buying them like crazy. Eventually Detroit got the hint. Now the American automakers hire the Japanese to make their engines, or they've copied their system. *Good Lemonade*, all over again."

We looked at a few more trucks; I don't think Mr. Everit ever really intended to buy one. Instead, he struck up a heartfelt talk with Carl about his life. Bert Everit was like an undercover therapist. He would connect with people, distract them from their troubles, and get them to talk about what was important to them. Then he would tell them he was sure they could have what they wanted, and leave them feeling better. I'll never forget the smile on Carl's face as he waved goodbye. He'd entirely forgotten that we didn't buy a truck.

Pretty soon Mr. Everit and I were sitting in rush hour traffic behind a school bus with kids making faces out of the back window. Mr. Everit made a face back, and the kids went wild.

"Your *Good Lemonade* idea reminds me of a restaurant near Santa Rosa," I told him.

"How's that?"

"One night while I was driving on a country road with my friend Denise, I noticed a big white house with a long line of cars parked down the lane. 'Quite a party those people are throwing!' I commented.

"'That's not a party,' Denise answered. 'It's a famous restaurant called *Theodore's*. Those cars belong to all the customers.'

"'But there's no sign on the restaurant,' I remarked. 'And it's out in the middle of nowhere.'

"'They've never had a sign,' she explained. 'They don't need one. The food is so good that people find out about it by word of mouth and figure out how to get here. The place is packed every night.'"

"So much for *'location! location!'*" Mr. Everit commented as he inserted a Celine Dion CD in the car player. "Word of mouth is the best sign and real estate you can invest in."

We sat in traffic long enough for Celine to sing us at least a dozen love songs. In the odd numbered songs, she found her true love. In the even numbered songs, she got dumped. Maybe she should see Dr. Phil, I wondered. Then we switched on the radio and happened on an NPR interview with a guy who had worked with Stephen Jobs when he started Apple Computers. "For Stephen," the fellow recounted, "no design issue was too small and it was never too late to do it right."

Was the universe trying to give me a message?

what I learned from Mr. Everit:

- Quality and integrity are the best advertising.
- If I take good care of people, life will take good care of me.
- Every business interaction is an opportunity to practice human connection.

Other stuff he said:

- Excellence is not an act, but a habit. (Aristotle)
- The more that he spoke of his honor, the faster we counted the spoons. (Emerson)
- Life is a succession of moments. To live each one is to succeed.

what I did:

- Made a commitment to myself to return phone calls and e-mails within 24 hours.
- Fixed or got rid of stuff in my apartment or office that doesn't work.
- Asked some of my coworkers how they were doing in their lives out of the office.

Worth It

For my birthday, Mr. Everit took me out for lunch to *Curry in a Hurry*, my favorite Indian restaurant. They rustle up *palak paneer* so spicy that steam shoots out of your ears. Taking me there was obviously an altruistic act, since he doesn't like hot food and they don't serve chocolate desserts.

On our way back to Big Buck, we passed a slick little boutique called *Sassy*. In the window I spied a sweater that got my attention in a big way. It was an ultra-lightweight blue and tan weave that looked masculine, yet fun. I stood there for a while eyeing it; I swear it had my name on it.

"Let's go in and have a look at it," Mr. Everit encouraged me as he opened the *Sassy* door. Reluctantly I followed and made my way to the window display. I turned over the price tag and read, "*$250.*" That was all I had to see. I dropped the tag and started to head back out to the street.

"Where do you think you're going, bucko?" Mr. Everit asked me, holding his hand over the door to bar me from passing.

"I don't really want it that much," I answered in a blasé tone. "Besides, those sweaters never look as good on people as they do on the mannequin."

"Oh, really?" he answered sarcastically. "Do your eyes always bulge out of your head when you're unimpressed?"

I tried to dislodge his hand from the door. "Do you know how many power tools I could buy for $250?" I shot back.

"Yes, I do," he answered, pressing his arm more firmly against the post. "But you can't wear a Skil Saw on a date. Not that many women are impressed by that."

Okay, okay.

He found an identical sweater on the shelf, held it up against my chest, and swiveled me around to look in the full-length mirror. The garment was indeed sassy. No cordless drill has ever done me such justice.

But facts were facts. "It's just too expensive," I pleaded. "I really can't justify paying this much for a sweater."

He looked me in the eye with that look I had gotten to know, the one that meant he was not kidding around. "I say you're worth it," he stated emphatically.

I wasn't thinking about the sweater that way. You buy stuff because you need it. If you have the money, you get it. If you don't, you leave it. That was my shopping formula. At least since I got serious about paying off my credit card bills.

He called the saleslady over. "Looks mighty good to me . . . Don't you agree?" asked Mr. Everit.

She smiled and nodded.

"But . . ." I began to object.

"I say you're worth it," he repeated. "I say you're worth having anything you love."

His message was starting to get to me. For a

moment I thought he was going to buy the sweater for me; I could see in his eyes that he was tempted. But I think he was trying to teach me a lesson I could learn only by doing it myself.

"Everything you buy is a statement of what you believe you're worth," he explained. "People who love and believe in themselves give themselves what makes them happy."

I kept staring at the sweater. It sure did look good.

"Well, when you put it like that . . . "

"We'll take it," he ordered the salesman.

What I learned from Mr. Everit:

· It's more fun to watch people enjoying themselves than to try to force them to do what I think they should do.

· Everything I purchase (and do) is a statement of what I believe I am worth.

· I am worth having anything I love.

Other stuff he said:

· If it's not a "Hell, yes!" it's a "Hell, no!"

· Give yourself abundant pleasure, so that you may have abundant pleasure to give others. (Neale Donald Walsch)

· You are not a beggar at the table of life. You are the honored guest. (Emmanuel)

What I did:

· Wore my new sweater to work.

· Gave away the clothes I once bought because they were cheap, yet hated every time I wore them because they reminded me I am poor.

· Went through my credit card statement and considered every purchase an investment in myself.

Lesson 8

Happy Money

The next afternoon I found Mr. Everit in his factory apartment watching an evangelist on cable TV. The fellow was alternately shouting and weeping, speaking in tongues, and asking for donations.

"Who does those guys' hair?" Mr. Everit muttered as he pressed the mute button on the remote. "You'd think that if God was speaking to them, He'd whisper a hint about those hairpieces." Then he sighed, "Oh, well, I guess Dominic has His ways . . ."

I chuckled, respectfully leaned back into John Lennon, and asked, "Why is it that so many religions teach that money is evil, and then spend so much time asking for it?"

"The church has to pay its mortgage, and the lenders won't accept prayers," he answered curtly.

"And what conclusion do you draw from that?"

"I don't come to conclusions. A conclusion is where you got tired of thinking. If I came to a conclusion, I'd be dead."

This was typical of the man. He would intrigue me and then leave me disoriented.

"Money is not the root of all evil," he stated

emphatically. "Ignorance is the root of all evil. People do cruel and foolish things for money because they feel oppressed by a sense of lack. If people knew their power to generate wealth, they would never fight or hurt each other over money."

I scratched my head and snidely answered, "That's easy for you to say. You have money."

Mr. Everit didn't flinch. He never did. "Money finds me because I enjoy it. I recognize it as a current of life and I love to keep it moving. If you wrap money in resentment, you will keep it at a distance. Call money good, and it will visit you often."

My mysterious mentor reached into his wallet, took out a dollar bill, and set it in front of me on the little round table under the lamp. As he removed the dollar, a small photo fell out of a side compartment and landed at my feet. Mr. Everit quickly leaned down to pick it up, but I reached it first. It showed a middle-aged bald Asian-looking man wearing a robe, maybe some kind of holy man. Next to him stood a younger tall white man with long hair, a scraggly beard, and wild eyes.

"Who is this?" I asked Mr. Everit.

He appeared nervous. "Can't you guess?" he returned quickly.

I looked more closely. The white guy looked familiar. I kept looking . . . Could it be? "That's not you, is it?" I asked him.

He smiled. "Good call."

"Whoa! . . . How old are you there? And what are you doing with that hair and beard?"

Mr. Everit took a breath and relaxed a little more, although he still seemed a bit edgy. "I was in my early twenties—it was the late sixties and I was into, well, you know, the hippie thing. Everybody had big hair in those days."

I still couldn't believe it was him. "And the guy with you?"

"That's Shin, a Buddhist monk I studied with. Very popular at that time."

Man, that picture threw me for a loop. Mr. Everit obviously felt embarrassed about it, and quickly stuffed the worn photo back into his wallet. Why he would carry it around all these years, I couldn't imagine. But I gathered he didn't want to talk about it, so I shifted the subject back to money. "Why'd you take out that dollar?"

Clearly relieved to be talking about that instead, he asked me, "Have you ever studied what's printed on a dollar bill?"

"Serial numbers?"

"Okay, wise guy. Have a look right here."

I leaned over and squinted to read.

"Right here it says, '*In God We Trust*,'" he pointed out. "Now there's a powerful affirmation! If every time you exchanged a dollar you remembered to trust God, or Dominic, or the universe, or whatever you want to call it, your money transactions would cease to be a source of irritation and become a blessing to you and everyone you work with."

I looked more closely at the symbols. The dollar was loaded with them: a pyramid, the all-seeing eye, a mystical key, and lots more. The originators of our currency were obviously tapped into some deeper wisdom that we've forgotten.

As I handed him back the dollar, Mr. Everit's secretary poked her head in the door. "Andrew Watson is on the phone from San Jose," she announced. "He doesn't want to pay the extra shipping cost we billed him for express service. He said regular would have worked."

Mr. Everit leaned back against his desk and folded his hands behind his head. "Then tell him to just deduct the extra charges from his invoice . . . We want only happy money."

There, he did it again. "What's 'happy money'?" I asked as soon as the secretary had gone.

"It's money exchanged by choice and with appreciation," Mr. Everit answered. "The giver believes the receiver deserves it, and pays willingly. Everybody walks away feeling good about the transaction."

"But you were just trying to help that outlet by shipping pronto," I reasoned. "You didn't have to give him a refund. Besides, our contract says that we ship at the method we deem best."

"You're absolutely right," he answered, folding the dollar back into his wallet. "But some rules run deeper than the ones on paper. There are times when engineering harmony is more important than being right. Over time, building relationships generates more revenue than holding people at gunpoint."

I could feel my indignation starting to well up. "But if you let people get away with things that aren't fair, you undermine your integrity."

Mr. Everit thought for a long moment and asked, "Do you want to know how I learned how 'happy money' works?" He rummaged through his Red Cloud box for a lone Peppermint Pattie, and then continued. "I stayed at a hotel that offered a 100 percent satisfaction guarantee. If there was anything you didn't like about your stay, you didn't have to pay."

"Well, that was pretty bold. I wonder how much money they lost on that promotion."

"So did I. I asked the hotel manager how many people took them up on it. 'Not many,' he told me. 'Less than one percent.' Then I understood what a brilliant business move that was. For the fewer than one out of a hundred people who asked for a refund, the company attracted half a dozen new customers who recognized the hotel's confidence and good will. That policy made the hotel a lot of money, not to mention consumer loyalty. Can you imagine the pride and satisfaction the manager felt to know that every penny of their income was paid with appreciation? What a great success model!"

"Yes, but there are always some people who will take advantage."

"Yes, some, but not enough to make a difference. On some level, everyone knows what is just, and most people are willing to pay fairly for goods and services."

"I don't know, Mr. Everit. I've seen lots of shady characters. What about people who loot during a disaster?"

"They are angry. Anger is fear under pressure. A sense of powerlessness drives people to act insanely and inhumanely. Those same people, if not incited, would show more integrity. I find it fascinating that when the twin towers were burning, no one in New York did any looting. People pulled together to help each other. That's how powerful we can be when we act out of strength, not fear."

"That may be true for some isolated incidents," I argued, "but don't you think that the larger a society grows, the more laws and safeguards we need to protect ourselves from people who would take advantage of others?"

"Both trust and mistrust are learned, and reinforce themselves with practice," he answered confidently. "The first time I checked into a hotel in Japan, I handed my credit card to the clerk. He politely returned it to

me and explained, 'You can pay when you check out.'
I was shocked! In America you need a credit check,
three bonded references, and a full body search just to
get a reservation in a trendy restaurant. In Japan they
simply trust you to pay on your way out. And people
do. People will act as honorable or crooked as you
treat them."

The more I tried to poke holes in Mr. Everit's
happy money theory, the more I realized he had
thought this out well. Even more compelling, his factory was a happy place. People smiled often, work got
done, and there was little employee turnover. Obviously his respect for his staff yielded very practical
results.

"It all comes back to your intentions," he
explained. "Is helping people at the top of your list of
business goals, or somewhere at the middle or bottom?" Then he gave me one of those point blank
looks and asked, "How much did you earn last year?"

I hesitated to answer. That was personal. Besides,
I was embarrassed. But then again, maybe he was trying to help me. "Maybe thirty-five grand," I answered.

"How many people's lives did you change for the
better?"

I had to think about that one. "I don't know . . .
some for sure . . . I couldn't tell you exactly."

"Then go home and think about it. When your
bottom line of how many people you helped trips off
your tongue as quickly as your balance sheet, you'll
understand happy money."

What I learned from Mr. Everit:

- Money is a current of energy that becomes good or evil depending on how you think of it and use it.

- If people knew their power to generate wealth, they would not need to force or withhold it from others.

- The only money worth having is that which is given and received with joy and choice.

Other stuff he said:

- The trouble with the rat race is that even if you win, you're still a rat. (Lily Tomlin)

- You can't get to heaven by putting other people through hell.

- Take care of people, and life will take care of you.

What I did:

- Gave Jesse Wilcox back the $100 I guilted him into giving me for the dent I found in my car that he swore he didn't do.

- Quit sending donations to organizations that send me unsolicited address labels I feel obligated to pay for.

- Made a list of the people I helped last year. This year it will grow.

Lesson 9

Make What You Want

At the end of May, Mr. Everit flew to Minneapolis to meet with some of our suppliers. He went on the road a couple of times a year, and always came home with so many presents you'd think he'd gone to Bora Bora. Maybe, I wondered on my way to pick him up at the airport, he was living out the family he never had. Or maybe he was just a generous fellow who wanted to enjoy his money while he could.

I caught sight of him on his way down the escalator; he never looked tired after his trips. As we approached baggage claim, I asked him how he stayed so calm. He scrunched his face like Yoda and answered in a gravelly voice, "*No try, only do.*" Then he laughed. "You know, like the butcher whose knife always stays sharp because he cuts around the gristle and never tries to fight through it."

No, I didn't know that butcher. All the butchers I knew had a lot of blood on their aprons.

On our way out of the airport parking lot, we found ourselves in a slow-moving line to pay the toll. I began to feel impatient. What was the big holdup?

Finally at the tollbooth we found a handsome

olive-skinned Italian man with thick white hair. As he handed us our change, he burst into several rousing verses from *La Traviata*. At first I thought he was a kook, but as he belted out the chorus, I noticed a rare sparkle in his eyes. He was enjoying himself immensely —and he wasn't a bad singer, either. When the toll man finished his performance, Mr. Everit and I smiled and applauded.

As we exited onto the state highway, Mr. Everit asked me, "Do you know what most people believe is the most boring job in the world?"

"Security guard?"

"Nope. *Toll collector*. I read it in a magazine."

He always seemed to have the facts he needed at his fingertips. Did he make them up?

"Do you think that toll collector back there was bored?" he asked me.

"Certainly not," I chuckled. "He was having a grand time."

"*Take what you have and make what you want*,'" Mr. Everit stated dryly.

"Take *what* . . . ?"

"Take what you have and make what you want," he repeated matter-of-factly. "It's the secret of happiness. Only a handful of people realize it. You just saw a living demonstration."

"That toll collector?"

"That man had supposedly 'the most boring job in the world'—and he was in heaven! A few hundred yards away, thousands of people with more money and mobility are hurrying and worrying. That man, in his tiny cubicle, refused to be stifled by his conditions. He took a dreary tollbooth in the thick of impatient drivers and smelly exhaust fumes, and turned it into an opera hall. I call that alchemy at its finest."

I looked back at the tollbooth, now just a dot in

the distance. There was still a line of cars waiting for their surprise concert.

"Do you think it's possible to do that with any job?" I asked. "Can you just take any job and make it work?"

"There are two ways you can change your life," he answered. "You can change your environment or you can change your mind. Sometimes you can change your environment. Always you can change your mind. It's the one thing you always have power over. Successful people find ways to shine right where they are."

If I smoked, I would have lit a cigarette. Instead, I reached for one of Mr. Everit's Skittles. We were quiet for a long while. Finally I asked him, "Does that mean we're supposed to stay in boring jobs or dead-end marriages?"

"Not at all," he shook his head, as if he knew exactly what I was going to ask. "It just means you're not supposed to tolerate situations that grate against your soul."

"So what do you do if you are stuck in some horrid situation you can't get out of?"

"You find ways to take care of yourself. I know a woman in Greece who was married for a long time to a nasty guy. When she asked him for a divorce, he refused. So she decided that if she had to stay, she would give herself the love she had been missing from him. Every day she wrote herself a love letter, like the one she wished an amorous man would send her. *'Dear Georgia, You are a beautiful, wise, precious, sensual goddess. I love you with all my heart and cherish you always.'* And on and on like that, for weeks."

"So where did that get her?"

"One day her husband found one of the letters. Since it was unsigned, he assumed it was from another man. He waved the letter in her face and told her, 'I can't compete with this . . . You can have your divorce!'"

Well, that would sure put a lot of divorce lawyers out of work right there.

"That woman literally loved herself out of a bad marriage," he added. "When she decided to source her own happiness, everything around her changed. Upgrading your life is an inside job. If you make cosmetic changes only, you're just rearranging chairs on the deck of a sinking ship."

That got me thinking. "Okay, then, try this on for size," I challenged him with faux confidence. He just looked at me with a half-raised eyebrow, like a veteran gunslinger toying with a cocky kid.

"I have to move at the end of this month. Last month I drove around town with a realtor and we found a house. It was small and in a noisy neighborhood, but since I'm under a time crunch, I told the realtor I would take it. He told me he would have the rental agreement drawn up and call me when it was ready.

"I didn't hear from him for a few weeks, so yesterday I phoned him and asked what was up. He sheepishly told me the landlord had decided not to rent to me because he wanted to rent to a member of his own religion.

"I was outraged. That's discrimination! Now I'll be stuck without a house soon. Do you think I should take him to court?"

Mr. Everit popped a Skittle and quietly answered, "I wouldn't waste my time."

"Why not?"

"Rejection is protection. If he doesn't want you there, believe me, you don't want to be there."

"But now I have to start all over."

He looked me dead in the eye. "Do you really think that landlord is the source of your supply?"

"What do you mean?"

"People think there is one mate, or one house, or one job they must have, and if they don't get it, they are ruined. That's ridiculous! No one person, place, or company is the source of your good. Life is the source of your good, and it has ingenious ways to deliver everything you need. The game board is much bigger than you realize."

Just then we were slowing down for a stoplight, the last one before Mr. Everit's house. "Hold up your hand," he ordered me.

Now what? "You want me to take some kind of oath?"

"No, I just want you to make sense of your life. . . . Hold up your hand and bend your index finger so it curls up into a tight 'C' shape."

I felt silly and made a face. But I did it anyway.

"Now look through the little pinprick of light in the middle and tell me what you see."

I looked, but could hardly see anything. "Not much," I told him.

"That's right," he concurred. "That's about as much as any of us sees on a good day. . . . Now gradually open your index finger and keep looking."

I went along with the game.

"What do you see now?"

"A lot more."

"Right. You just got the Big Picture. It was there even while you were seeing only a tiny piece of the puzzle."

"Is this some kind of trick?"

"Not nearly as tricky as your mind when it tells you you're powerless," he asserted. "When you thought you had to have that one house, you were looking through the pinprick crack. Opening your finger is like recognizing the Big Picture. Quit telling

Dominic how to engineer your success. Just relax, do what you can where you can, and watch for signs."

By then we were pulling into Mr. Everit's driveway. As he got out of the car he told me, "Be glad you didn't get that house—jeez, you didn't even like it, anyway!" Then he turned and headed for his front door.

I just sat there shaking my head, as usual.

On my way home I felt like taking a back road; I figured the country scenery would clear my head. Along the way I noticed a house with a *For Rent* sign on the lawn. On a whim, I parked and inquired. The landlady was happy to show me the place. It was in a quiet area, had lots of room, the rent was less expensive than the place that had fallen through, and it was ten minutes from the factory. And she was delighted at the prospect of renting to me. The house was perfect in every way. I rented it on the spot, and later moved in with time to spare.

It seems that the universe was conspiring to take care of me, in spite of my efforts to tell it how.

what I learned from Mr. Everit:

- I can make anything out of anything.

- If I can't change a situation, I can reframe it in my mind so it works in my favor.

- No single person or company is the source of my good. My source is infinite, and can find me in ways I haven't even thought of.

Other stuff he said:

- When the defining moment comes along, you define the moment or the moment defines you.

(From the movie Tin Cup)

- Struggle to get, struggle to keep.

- For a web begun, God sends thread.

(Inscribed on the ceiling of the U.S. Library of Congress.)

what I did:

- Painted my office a color I liked. I didn't care if anyone else approved. I was the one who had to live with it.

- Wrote a love letter to myself. (At least I have one fan.)

- Made a small poster and pasted a reminder on the edge of my desk:

Remember the Big Picture.

Lesson 10

Easy Does It

The next morning I was swamped at work from the minute I walked in the door. The phone kept ringing, my e-mail inbox was glutted, and some jackhammer idiot picked my window to work under. Finally I got fed up and escaped to Mr. Everit's office, where I found him tearing an order form out of a catalog of odd inventions. He proudly showed me a photo of *The Ultimate Back-Scratching T-Shirt*, which sported a sort of bingo grid printed on the back, and came with a small matching card. "This way when Marlene scratches my back, I won't have to keep saying, 'more up and to the left,'" he exclaimed as if he had just discovered the Rosetta Stone. "I can just tell her, 'C-7.'"

Whatever.

I eagerly told Mr. Everit how I had found my new place. He shook my hand vigorously and said, "You just mastered the lesson that would save most people many years of hardship, if they could just grasp it."

"What's that?"

"*Let it be easy.* When you lighten up and follow your intuition, you are guided to where you need to be. It was no accident that you felt like taking that back road home—your internal pilot led you impeccably. Now you just have to trust that sense and act on it as much as you can. Then you'll achieve your goals at light speed, while other people around you are duking it out because they think life is a contest."

Again Mr. Everit was refuting much of what I had been taught about how to succeed. "But isn't struggle a necessary element of life?" I asked brashly. "You know, 'survival of the fittest'?"

"'The fittest' are not necessarily those with the most muscles and meat. The real fittest are those who can best fit into what is called for in any given situation. Dinosaurs were big and strong, but they were also dumb and inadaptable—"

"—and so are lots of people, still."

"Granted. But wisdom and compassion ultimately prevail over bully tactics. People who rely on strong-arming may make short-term gains, but they eventually shoot themselves in the foot. Ever read *The Darwin Awards*? Like the guy who was trying to shake a free soda out of a Coke machine, until it fell over and squashed him?"

Sure, I'd read *The Darwin Awards*. People with pea brains canceling themselves out of the gene pool.

"But a lot of people in the business world aren't much more evolved than that dimwit," I remarked. "Instead of shaking a Coke machine, they're cutting each others' throats."

"And they're miserable," he added. "Don't be fooled by their Porsches and slinky girlfriends. You can't cut someone else's throat and leave your own intact." Mr. Everit paused for a moment, rubbed his chin thoughtfully, and asked, "Do you know the day and time of week when most people die?"

"When they open their credit card statement?"

"Nope. Monday morning at 9 A.M. I read that in a medical statistics book. It tells me that most people would rather drop dead than go to work."

I wasn't surprised. "So are we doomed to trudge through life like mules in quicksand and die a little bit more every day, until we finally just keel over?"

He shook his head. "Nobody's doomed to do anything. We doom ourselves by putting up with lives smaller than we are."

"Well, that sounds noble, Bert, but it's cold out there in the corporate world. You have to make a lot of compromises and bust your chops to stay afloat. It's a heartless jungle—I know, I've been there."

"C'mere," he urged, motioning me to follow him down the hall to his apartment. He fluffed the pillows on his little couch and invited me to sit down in front of the TV. Then he began to rummage through a bunch of videotapes in a faded Thom McCann shoebox under the set.

"With all its fierceness, nature has compassion built into its fiber," he announced over his shoulder. "Do you remember that news story about the gorilla in the zoo near Chicago?"

"Not really."

"It's an eye-opener," he swore, still poking through the box. "I was watching the news one night and . . . Ah! Here it is."

Like a little boy eager to show me his prize baseball card, Mr. Everit inserted the cassette into the player. Someone just happened to be videotaping the gorilla section at the Brookfield Zoo when a three-year-old boy climbed over the retaining wall and plummeted seventeen feet onto the concrete floor below. The child hit his head and fell unconscious in the midst of a group of gorillas. The boy's mother went hysterical, while shocked onlookers ran to summon zoo officials. Before anyone could get to the boy, a gorilla named Binti Jua, with her own infant clinging to her back, brushed away the other gorillas and took the unconscious child in her arms. She tenderly carried the boy to the door of the gorilla cage and handed him to an attendant. Later that year, a national magazine named Binti Jua "Humanitarian of the Year."

"That's amazing!" I had to admit.

"No more amazing than what the most hard-headed manager can do if he gets his head out of his butt and into his heart."

"But what about the 'no pain, no gain' idea?" I challenged him. "That poster was plastered in the locker room of every school I attended."

"I know," he echoed, rubbing his hand in a circle over his belly. "I sure have gained!" he laughed. "'No pain, no gain' is a half-truth," he added more seriously. "Sure, you learn from pain, but you also learn through ease and fun—sometimes even more effectively. When you are learning to ride a bike, you learn from falling off, but you learn just as much—maybe more—when you stay balanced and enjoy the ride. Pain has a purpose, but it is highly overrated as a teaching device. If you pay attention to internal signals and external feedback, life won't need a two-by-four to get your attention."

This all seemed too easy. "But if people took it easier, we'd drift toward a lazy, nonproductive society."

"Don't be so sure. My buddy Hal Moskowitz got pretty stressed out running a big plumbing supply chain. So he hired a personal coach to help him keep his sanity and his job, not to mention his health. The coach convinced Hal to take one day out of his work-week to just do things he found relaxing. So he went to the beach, played golf, and took his dogs for long walks in the park. Soon Hal found that the ideas and creativity he generated during that one day a week, without even trying, made his four-workday week far more productive and enjoyable than when he had been working five days. He is now a full-blown convert to creative relaxation."

By then our conversation had drifted onto Mr. Everit's little patio. It felt good to just kick back with him, especially after escaping from desk hell. He brought me a cold Dr. Pepper and a bowl of fudge mint cookies. Just as we got settled, a baby blue BMW Z-4 convertible rounded the only corner we could see. We watched what looked like a mother and her daughter each talking on their own cell phones. The scene looked straight out of Beverly Hills; we chuckled.

"Take cell phones," he suggested. "Great inventions. When I first got mine, I didn't own it—it owned me. Until one morning when I was sitting at breakfast at the Ambassador Hotel with some friends, I got a business call. I got so wrapped up in the conversation that I didn't taste a bite of my omelet or enjoy my friends. When we parted, I realized I had missed out on being with them. I had wasted precious minutes of my life. That was a big turning point for me. Now it's life first, cell phone second. I don't care how many rainbow-colored interchangeable flashing face plates they offer me."

I thought about my cousin Laura, who would have her cell phone surgically injected in her ear if she could. She hasn't finished a meal since 1997.

"All of our time- and labor-saving devices are wonderful," he went on, "but what do you do with the extra time these gadgets net you? Do you use the time for things that make your life more rewarding, or do you just fill the time with more stuff you have to do? Far as I can tell, the only real measure of success is happiness. What good are all the trendy toys if your soul gets run over along the way?"

"I'm not in the market for trendy toys," I interjected sarcastically. "I'd be happy to just get my bills paid. You might as well just make out my paycheck to Citibank Visa."

"Good point. Wherever you are is where you start. The next time you get stressed, ask yourself, 'How would I be doing this differently if I were willing to let this be easy?' So you pay your bills, but don't let them rob your happiness. Think of someone you know who is relaxed, and consider how they might approach the same task."

I thought of my Uncle Sandor. The guy didn't let anything get him down; he just took everything in stride. He had a bumper sticker on his car that said, *"Too blessed to be stressed."*

"There is always a next level of relaxation you can go to in any situation," Mr. Everit went on. "Ask yourself what that would be, and you'll start to go there."

"Even when that world-class witch Shirley Jackman from accounting calls me to vent? Lord, you'd think I was her primal scream therapist!"

Mr. Everit rolled his eyes; she bugged him, too. "You may have to take it, but you don't have to take it personally," he replied. "Just remember it's not about you. If she's all whacked out and you stay clear, you are in a far stronger position to handle the situation. Nasty people are disconnected. When you stay connected, you emerge triumphant."

"And when I have three phones ringing at once . . . ?"

"Just because technology lets you do twelve things at a time, doesn't mean you have to. Spin as many plates as you can without them crashing on you. If you can fully give your attention to one thing at a time, everything you do will speak of excellence."

There, he had me again. I took a breath and *easily* made my way back to my office.

What I learned from Mr. Everit:

- Ease is a more effective success attitude than struggle.
- My intuition is wise—I just have to listen to it.
- There is always a next level of relaxation I can go to in any situation.

Other stuff he said:

- There's a reason people don't have pictures of their office at home.
- Before you climb the ladder of success, be sure you have it set against the right wall.
- The hours that make us happy make us wise. (John Masefield)

What I did:

- Took my lunch hour at the lake rather than eating at my desk.
- Turned my cell phone off when I am with people I value.
- Ordered the Ultimate Back-Scratching T-Shirt as an act of faith that I would find someone to help me use it.

Happy and Hungry

On the first day of summer, Mr. Everit invited me to his house to kick off the swimming pool season. The sun felt ever so good as we sat poolside, casually munching on a small mountain of nachos while Marlene floated aimlessly on a pontooned lounge chair, sipping a frosty margarita, immersed in *Cosmopolitan*. I was lost in a Dave Mathews CD on my Discman when I felt a tap on my shoulder. I pulled off my headset and sat up, to find Bert holding a copy of *USA Today*.

"You have to see this," he nudged me, handing me the paper and pointing to a small illustration of a yellow smiley face. "The newspaper did a survey asking highly successful people which came first: happiness or success?"

"And they didn't include me in the survey?" I asked, indignant.

He shook his head. "Well, there's no accounting for taste."

"Oh, alright . . . . What did they find?"

"Sixty-three percent said they were successful because they were happy. Thirty-seven percent said they were happy because they were successful."

Hmmmm. "And which category do you fit into, Mr. Everit?"

"It's a no-brainer," he answered, pausing to down an especially hot chip. "If your happiness depends on success, any little setback will plunge you into upset. Then you bob up and down like a cork on a squally ocean." He made a funny bobbing motion with his head and curled his lips as if he was woozy. "People who decide to be happy no matter what the stock market is doing, find all kinds of things to feel successful about—and attract more."

Then he shrugged his shoulders and stated, "I don't need any more money . . . I have enough."

His statement jarred me; I'd never heard anyone say they had enough money. Even the wealthiest people I know always need more. Some of the few millionaires I've met were bigger whiners than people on food stamps. It seems that people who think they don't have enough, never get it, and people who think they have enough, never miss it.

"You're really satisfied with what you have?" I asked, incredulous. "Don't you want to get richer?"

"I'm already rich," he answered authoritatively. "In fact, I'm the richest man in the world."

What? "Oh, come on, now, Mr. Everit, I know you have a few bucks in the bank, but you're no Bill Gates or Oprah."

He smiled. "Of course I'm no billionaire. If you define riches by money, I'm just an average Joe. But if you consider the immense good in my life, I am loaded. I have a loving wife . . . a fulfilling job . . . friends I laugh with . . . magnificent sunsets . . . inspiring books . . . music that feeds my soul. Sure, I have my challenges, but they help me get stronger. If I start to go into a funk, I remember how blessed I am, and things shift. And now you're here. What more could any man ask for?"

He leaned back and took a deep thoughtful breath. "No sir, Bill and Oprah don't have a thing over Bert Everit," he declared. "When it comes to true wealth, I'm richer than a king."

There was not a thing I could say to that. Bert Everit had found the riches so many seek, but so few find. I began to consider that I, too, might have enough without even realizing it. Maybe I was doing better than I thought.

He read my mind again. "'Enough' is not a number or condition to be attained," he explained. "It's an attitude you cultivate. Most people go to great pains to decide how they will invest their money, but think little about how they are investing their thoughts, which are more crucial. They spend most of their attention on the one thing that went wrong, and overlook the thousand things that went right. They don't realize that you get more of whatever you focus on."

"So everyone on the planet is living in their own reality, and we all just keep finding evidence to prove what we believe?"

"Couldn't have said it better myself," he echoed, passing the nachos toward me. "Take your basic supermodel, for example. People 'ooh' and 'aah' over her perfect body wherever she goes. But she's never quite beautiful enough for herself. She is terrorized by the tiniest wrinkle, wart, or sag. She lives on one lettuce leaf a day and purges if she eats a doughnut. Constant fear and anxiety. A self-critical mind in a perfect body translates to one hell of a life."

I'd never thought of it like that before. I always envied gorgeous women or handsome men; I figured they had it made.

"By contrast, when Marlene and I visited a beach on the Black Sea, you wouldn't believe the condition of some of those bodies on display! More like *National Enquirer* than *Vogue*! Men with surgical scars longer than Amtrak, and women with breasts sagging halfway to Albania. Yet they just march around topless and in little bikinis, as if they were Julia Roberts! I must say I was quite impressed by their relaxed attitude. A self-accepting mind in an imperfect body translates to one wonderful day at the beach."

Okay, I got the idea. "But if everybody just accepted everything as it is, we'd never get anywhere," I argued. "There'd be no striving for improvement. Isn't it important to stretch for more? To set goals beyond your current level of attainment?"

"Exactly! Just don't be disappointed if you never get everything done. On the day you die, you will have e-mail in your inbox."

Now there was a sobering thought.

"There's as much fun in going as getting there," he insisted. "You will never wake up one day, wipe your hands clean, and declare, 'There, that's it! I'm done.' There will always be more that you want or have to do. Like the Lexus ad that asked, *'Why pursue perfection when you can drive it?'* Lots of people are pursuing perfection; very few are driving it. You don't need a Lexus to drive perfection; you just need to decide to enjoy the ride."

"So we don't need to die and go to heaven to be happy?"

"Hell, no!" he bellowed. "Heaven is not a place you end up. It is a sense of joy right where you are. We all thrive on movement, color, contrast, and new stimulation. Honestly, how long could you lie on some cloud and listen to harp music? I'd go buggy after half an hour!"

I had to laugh; he had a point. "So the process of reaching for perfection is part of perfection?"

"Absolutely. We can appreciate what we have while striving for better. The two are not mutually exclusive. We can live 'happy and hungry.'"

Happy and hungry. I'd not thought of those two on the same playing field. A few people I know are happy. Most are hungry.

A strange question occurred to me. "Are you really happy, Mr. Everit?" I blurted out. Suddenly I feared I had overstepped my boundaries. But it was too late. Might as well ask what I really wanted. "Do you ever get afraid or depressed?"

Bert Everit was silent for what was probably just a few seconds, but seemed like ten minutes to me. Then he nodded, "Sure . . . like you, I am a work in progress."

"You always seem so upbeat and together. Sometimes I wonder if you make mistakes."

"Good Lord," he laughed. "Everything I know is a result of the mistakes I've made! I've messed up so many times that I'm an expert in what not to do! Mistakes have been my greatest teachers."

Then Mr. Everit grew somber and uncharacteristically averted his eyes from mine. I'd never seen him look so rattled before. If I didn't know him better, I'd swear I saw a small tear well up in the corner of his eye.

"Are you alright?" I asked him.

He did his best to regain his composure, but I could tell something was bothering him.

"I'll be fine," he answered curtly. "You just reminded me of a mistake I made a long time ago— one I'm still trying to rectify."

"What was that?"

He thought for a moment, obviously wrestling with himself. "It's not something I can talk about right now," he answered. "One day I'll tell you."

It was the strangest thing he had ever said to me. I decided to just leave it at that.

what I learned from Mr. Everit:

- Happiness is not something that happens to you. It's an attitude you cultivate.

- If you feel rich, you are. There are lots of riches besides money.

- Wanting more is healthy and natural. Just don't forget to enjoy what you have.

Other stuff he said:

- Why get rich quick when you can be rich now?

- There are only two ways to live your life: One is as though nothing is a miracle. The other is as though everything is a miracle. (Einstein)

- A visionary thrives under all conditions.

What I did:

- Wrote a list of reasons why I have enough.

- Wrote a list of reasons why I want and deserve more.

- Put both papers on the desk in front of me, and stared at them until the knot in my stomach loosened.

The Faithkeeper

"Mr. Everit, our system's crashed!" Janie Hampton shrieked down the hall. Just what we needed the morning after Fourth of July vacation, when summer sales were peaking. Mr. Everit had warned me how busy summer would get, and he wasn't kidding. Now this. Why did things go wrong just when they were going right?

I dashed out of my office and followed Mr. Everit to the comptroller's desk. Our computer wizard, Tony Rowe, was tinkering with the system and getting no results. Pretty soon folks in all the offices were getting itchy. No one could access any data, and we were losing orders by the minute.

"Have you called Lenny Stillwell?" Mr. Everit asked Janie. "If he programmed our system, he can fix it."

"His office said he's on vacation in Cancun," she reported, shaking her head. "No telling when they'll be in touch with him."

"Then try some other computer people. We'll find someone."

Without a word, Mr. Everit turned and headed

toward the employee lounge. I tagged along behind him, hoping for more commentary. "Aren't you worried?" I asked him. "This could back up everything for days!"

He held the lounge door for me and replied, "Actually, I know a guy who proved that worrying works."

"Really? How did he do that?"

"He wrote down everything he worried about, and none of it came true."

Got me.

Mr. Everit glided to the vending machine and bought a Snickers bar. "Would you like to know how I got over worrying?" he asked over his shoulder.

"I'd gladly give you my paycheck."

"That won't be necessary," he answered. "Once you know, you'll be worth twice your salary."

He pulled his chair next to mine, took a long gooey bite out of his Snickers, and began flipping through an automotive magazine lying on the table. He paged through it for a long time without saying a word. I began to wonder if he had forgotten what we were talking about. Maybe Mr. Everit's burritos were starting to unravel.

Finally he blurted out, "Ah!" and turned the magazine to me, pointing to a car ad. "That, my friend, is the new Thunderbird."

I studied the car. Very slick.

"These new T-birds are a resurrection of the original classic model. Would you be very impressed to know that I owned one?"

"May I touch you?"

"No, you may listen, since what I am about to tell you could save you a lifetime of angst, not to mention considerable therapy and Prozac bills—if you can just get over your flaw of irreverence."

"Okay, okay."

He leaned in as if he was going to make confession to a priest. "I owned my T-bird for five years and babied it like a child star. When I married Marlene, we couldn't fit us and her Golden Retriever Sadie in the bucket seats, so the car had to go. Mind you, I hated to part with it—but you gotta do what you gotta do. So I put an ad in the *Clarion*, and an interested woman called. We made an appointment to meet the next afternoon in the parking lot of a local restaurant. I took my baby to be detailed, and man, she cleaned up real nice."

Was this a car, or a woman?

"As I drove to meet the buyer, the car radio started pulsing on and off. I looked at the voltage meter on the dashboard and saw the needle dropping rapidly. My electrical system was shutting down."

"On your way to sell the car?"

"Within *minutes* of selling the car—and I'd never had a problem with it until then!"

"Sounds like some strange movie plot."

"Wait—it gets only stranger. Knowing that engine failure was imminent, I prayed to at least make it to the parking lot where the woman was waiting. Then the unbelievable happened: The moment I entered the lot, the car died and I literally rolled into the parking spot next to the one where she was waiting."

"No way! What did you tell her?"

"Before I could say anything, she started chewing me out. I was late and she was going to be late for work. I thought I was on time, but the car's electrical failure had slowed down its clock by twenty minutes."

"Are you making this up?"

"I wish I were. After she pushed her veins back in

her neck, Miss Huffy asked to take the car for a test drive. I swear, if I could have come up with a good lie, I would have. But I couldn't. So I just confessed, 'I hate to tell you this, but the car just died.'"

Very bizarre.

"'What do you mean "died?"' she barked. 'Didn't you just drive it in here?'

"'Yes, I did,' I answered sheepishly, 'but the engine gave out a few seconds ago . . . something with the electrical system.'

"She made this weird look with her face, like she was constipated, and then grunted, 'Well . . . call me when you get it fixed!' Then she stomped into her car and peeled out in a huff."

"So what did you do?"

"What could I do? I called a tow truck. An hour later I watched my beautiful T-bird—flawless until that day—being dragged along the highway like a side of beef. I just sat there thinking, 'This is too weird to be true.' I told myself this was just a momentary set-back. I would get the car fixed, someone would buy it, and, when all the dust settled, this incident wouldn't matter much."

"And did it?"

"I got the car fixed easily enough—the problem was just a broken belt—and the T-bird sat in my garage for a few weeks while I was away on a business trip. When I returned, I took a long shot and phoned my frustrated buyer. 'Are you still interested in the car?' I asked.

"She was calmer now. 'Well, I guess so,' she answered. 'You'll never believe what happened while you were away. I looked at two other cars, and they both failed when I tried them.'

"What, I ask you, are the odds of that happening? Anyway, she took the T-bird for a spin, loved it, and paid me a good price for it. I delivered the car to her with a flower and greeting card wishing her well. A month later she sent me a thank-you note telling me how much she loved the T-bird."

Okay, we were on a final approach to the point. "And that taught you to stop worrying?"

"The defining moment came when I was sitting in the tow truck and realized that this was all going to get handled. I didn't know how, but I figured it would. And it did."

"Like that character in *Shakespeare in Love* who would keep getting into jams and say, 'Somehow it will work out!' And it did."

Just then Janie dashed into the lounge. "We've got Lenny Stillwell on the phone," she announced excitedly. "He just happened to call his office from Cancun. He's talking to Tony, walking him through correcting the crash. It looks like we have it handled . . . can you believe that timing?"

I wasn't *that* surprised. Mr. Everit had called it.

"There really is a design to the universe," Mr. Everit stated as he kept poring over the T-bird ad. "You just have to move with the strongest energy."

"You mean, like, 'go with the flow?'"

"It's more than that. You help the flow, even create it, by keeping your goal foremost in your mind and not letting yourself be distracted by appearances to the contrary. Anchor yourself in your objective, and obstacles will evaporate as you walk through them." Mr. Everit opened the venetian blinds and let a welcome waft of sunlight into the lounge. His regal silhouette grew pronounced, and for a moment I could have been watching a great statesman at his palatial window.

"I saw a TV show about a Native American medicine man," he told me. "The show was called 'The Faithkeeper.' His job in the tribe was to remain at peace no matter what happened around him or the tribe. When other people were falling prey to fear, he was the rock of strength. If there was bad weather, disease, war, or shortage of any kind, he had to hold the vision that his tribe would come out on the other side. And they did."

On the table before me was a copy of the morning newspaper. I read the headlines. Yuck. War, murder, economic downturn, scandal, epidemics, and on, and on, and on. "I guess we could use some more faithkeepers in our tribe," I commented.

"That would be you," he smiled wryly.

what I learned from Mr. Everit:

- Life is guided by an intelligence that matches people with the things they need.

- There is a part of me that is clear and strong, even when other parts are not. In a crisis, my best move is to let that part lead.

- Somehow everything works out.

Other stuff he said:

- Worry is like a rocking chair. It gives you the feeling you are doing something, but you don't get anywhere.

- As soon as you trust yourself, you will know how to live. (Goethe)

- Nothing in life is to be feared. It is only to be understood. (Madame Curie)

What I did:

- Made a list of stuff I was worried about. Then I wrote after each item, "Somehow this will work out."

- Didn't rush to get into the first boarding group on my Southwest flight. I got in the group anyway and got a great seat.

- Told my mom I was gonna be all right.

Lesson 13

Don't Ration Your Passion

"Your birthday?" I asked when I saw the field of Mylar balloons on his desk.

"Twenty-five years," he answered proudly.

"You're only twenty-five?" I asked. "You seem more, uh . . . seasoned . . . than that."

"Twenty-five years since I became factory manager," he laughed, playfully flicking one of the balloons. "Doin' anything tonight?"

"Uh, let's see . . . I cancelled my meeting with the president—I'm tired of giving him advice . . . I guess I'm free."

"Then how about celebrating with me at a concert? Marlene was gonna go, but she has to go to remedial driving school. A cop stopped her for speeding, and she told him he was creating his own reality."

What I would have given to be there.

"What kind of concert? . . . Heavy metal? . . . Hip-hop? . . . Rap?"

"Close . . . violin."

"Seriously?"

"Have I ever steered you wrong?"

No, he certainly hadn't. "Okay, I'm in. . . . Just don't let me down, alright?"

"You won't be sorry."

I wasn't. I'm not into classical music, but this soloist was phenomenal. She made love to those strings with fervor that made me giggle at first, then drew tears, and finally set the hall on fire. I must have been the first in the audience to jump to my feet and yell, "*Bravo!*"

After the concert, on our way to Bennigan's-Where-They-Have-a-Chocolate-Decadence-Dessert, Mr. Everit asked me, "Did you read in the program how that musician got her violin?"

I never read those things. "And how was that?"

"She was in the market for a violin and found a genuine Stradivarius. The price was far beyond any money she had. She figured that the only way she could buy the violin would be to sell her house."

"So what did she do?"

"She sold her house."

"She sold her whole house for that violin?"

"Far as I can tell, it was a good deal," he elbowed me. "I doubt she could ever get such good music out of her house." Probably not. "Now she's making enough money to buy a nicer house than the one she traded for the fiddle."

At Bennigan's we sat in a booth next to a bunch of kids who had just gotten out of a movie. One guy had so many tattoos, he could have been a roadmap of the L.A. freeway system. That was just his forearm; I dared not even consider where the 405 ended up.

"Frankly, I'm surprised I enjoyed the concert as much as I did," I admitted as we handed our menus back to the waitress. "I don't know anything about classical music."

"You don't have to," Mr. Everit responded. "Do you know what kind of music elicits the strongest reaction in listeners?"

"Country and western?" I guessed.

"Why would you say that?"

"It makes a few people cry and everyone else hurl."

"Good try . . . but get this: Some psychologists hired a bunch of different musicians to play various kinds of music for a live audience, and they measured their responses."

"And they found . . . ?"

"They found that no particular kind of music creates more of a response than another. Can you guess what made the biggest difference?"

"The ticket price?"

"Nope. The state of mind of the musician. The musicians who played with the most passion turned the audience on the most."

"Seriously?"

"People respond more to feelings than technique. That's the power of passion."

I'd never really thought about it like that.

"And do you want to know a secret that's not really a secret, but nobody knows it, so it might as well be?"

"What's that?"

"Playing with passion is not just the key to music. It's the key to everything."

"Like that toll collector who sang opera?"

"Exactly. If you can find the guts to do what you are passionate about, people will pay you to feel the energy you breathe into your creations."

"Even, like, quilting?"

"A quilt made with passion is the finger of God reaching into life to touch the souls of everyone who looks upon it."

"So you're suggesting I take up the violin or quilting?"

He laughed. "I am suggesting that you take up being yourself. If you live from your passion, you will be happy, successful, bring gifts to the world, and be amply rewarded."

"And this would work for everyone?"

"Even engineers."

"But, if everyone has such gifts, why aren't more people happy and successful?"

"They don't believe that greatness lives within them. If they believed in themselves enough to do what they love, life would rush to support them."

"So it's not outrageous to do what I want?"

"The only thing more outrageous than doing what you want is settling for what you don't want."

Suddenly something clicked inside me. I got what Mr. Everit was telling me. Not just about the violinist, or quilting, or passion. About everything. I got the Big Picture. Somehow my life was an expression of perfection, even if I couldn't explain how. The universe embodied a vast wisdom that could deliver all of my dreams to my doorstep, if I just got out of my own way and let life love me. And it all began with me saying yes—to myself, to every experience that brought me to where I now stand, to everything. I was as rich as Mr. Everit and everyone who discovered gold right where they lived. I already had enough, and I could have more. I was happy and I was hungry.

I just sat there for a minute or two, staring at Mr. Everit, but more staring through him. Then he threw me the biggest curveball of all.

"While we're on the subject of passion, I have to tell you that I have decided to follow my passion."

"You mean you haven't been following it all along?"

"Of course I have. Now I am simply following it to my next step. I'm leaving the factory."

I could hardly believe my ears. "Leaving the factory? . . . Mr. Everit, you *are* the factory. If you left, it would all fall apart!"

He guffawed. "Now that wouldn't say much about me or the company, would it? I haven't trained all these people for all these years to depend on me. I hope I've taught them to be self-igniting."

This was too bizarre. "But you are the master. Who among us could manage as well as you?"

"You could."

"*Me?*"

"That's right—you."

"Oh, come on, Mr. Everit. I don't have what it takes to be like you."

"But you have what it takes to be like you. That's all that matters."

My head was spinning. "I don't know, Mr. Everit. Sometimes I wonder if you see who I really am."

Then he looked way into me, silently, for a long time. It was a little scary. "I see who you are more than you see who you are," he told me in a strong voice. "That's why I'm turning the company over to you."

I sank into my seat, trying to take it all in. There was no use arguing. He knew what he wanted, and he was usually right.

"You can have my office, my apartment, my salary, my assistant. Everything I have is yours."

I just sat there, completely befuddled. "And what are you going to do? Retire?"

He burst out in laughter so raucous that the tattoo people in the next booth turned and stared. I shrank back against the booth.

"Me? Retire? Now there's a good joke! Can you

imagine me playing golf in plaid pants with a bunch of old fogies in Arizona? That's not my idea of heaven, my friend. That's right up there with the clouds and harp music. I'm in life for the distance."

A glimmer shot from his eyes. "Marlene and I are taking a few months to go to the Mediterranean. She's always wanted to see Athens and Madrid, and I intend to wow her at every turn. I want the rest of the time in our life to be more meaningful than searching for the remote."

Then he got that look on his face, that strange look he had gotten once before when he told me about the big mistake he had made, the one he couldn't tell me about. "There are things I want her to know about me that I need some time to talk about. I think it will be good for both of us."

Again I felt that I would be treading into unwelcome territory if I said even a word.

"And when we get back, there are some things I want to talk with you about. Things that will help you to hear."

"What things?" I asked myself. "Why couldn't he tell me now?" But he was done for now, I could tell. And when he was done, he was done.

I grabbed the check. I figured that now I could afford it.

What I learned from Mr. Everit:

- People will pay me to feel the passion and energy I breathe into my career and creations.

- I can't afford to do anything with less than a whole heart.

- I can retire from a career, but never life.

Other stuff he said:

- Chase your passion, not your pension. (Denis Waitley)

- Let the beauty we love be what we do. (Rumi)

- Before you die, dare to walk the wildest unknown way. (Bryce Courtney)

What I did:

- Quit the Young Executives Club. I was bored there.

- Got out my camera, which I haven't used for years—but always love when I do.

- Made a list of changes in the factory that I would make if I were manager. Holy Bert, I **am** the manager.

Lesson 14

A Better Deal

I looked up at my *Great Chocolates of Europe* calendar that Mr. Everit had sent me from Switzerland, and could hardly believe that he and Marlene had been gone for nearly two months. In a week I would be the factory manager picking them up at the airport, and they would be the visitors. What a weird turnaround in less than a year! I wondered if he had had his meaningful talk with his wife. Everyday I wondered what he would say to me when he came home.

At first I had tried to step into Mr. Everit's shoes, but quickly I realized that he was the only one who could fill them. If I was going to succeed, it would have to be on my own terms. Besides, Bert Everit would never stand for a clone. For the first month he was away, I asked myself, "What would Mr. Everit do?" Then I began to consider, "What would *I* do?"

In spite of my fears and insecurity, the factory workers carried on admirably. Mr. Everit's absence forced everyone to think for themselves, and the place hummed along at a new level of pride and efficiency. His employees proved his point that the mark of a good leader is the success of his protegés in his absence. "A good teacher seeks to make himself unnecessary," he used to say. Truly the factory's increased productivity was a feather in Mr. Everit's cap.

Nothing, however, could have prepared me for the phone call from Mr. Everit's nephew, Jason. It came just before lunch on the Tuesday before Thanksgiving. I was making some notes on the final draft of the new company catalog, hoping that Mr. Everit would be impressed when he saw it. My secretary had just gone to lunch, so I answered the phone myself.

"I'm afraid I have some bad news," Jason began. I braced myself. "Marlene just called and told me that Uncle Bert had a heart attack while scuba diving off the coast of Greece. They took him to a local hospital, where they kept him on life support. He was coherent for a few days, and then had another heart attack. They couldn't save him. . . . He's gone."

"God, no . . ."

"Didn't you know about his heart condition?"

"No—he never said anything about it."

Jason paused for a moment and took a deep breath. "Eleven years ago Uncle Bert had a heart attack. His doctor told him never to scuba dive again. But he did. He loved it. He used to take me and my brother diving every month. We loved it, too. I guess he just pushed it too far this time."

So that was Mr. Everit's mysterious secret. It wasn't so weird. I wondered why he never told me. Did he have too much pride?

After we hung up, I sat and thought for a long time. Bert Everit was not coming home. The last time I saw him was the last time I would ever see him. How could that be? The bottom of my stomach dropped out. Then the tears started to well up and I shut the door to my office. I let my head fall back onto my chair and stared at the ceiling for a long time through wet eyes. In my mind I went over all of our times together, from the day I showed up at the factory, to his last wink to me at the airport. He had grown to mean so much to me; I couldn't begin to count the many doors he had opened. He saw more in me than I saw in myself, and I caught his vision. In his own strange way, he had dismantled my rickety little wheelbarrow and replaced it with one big enough to hold all my heart's desires.

Now he was gone.

It was as if he knew what was going to happen when he turned everything over to me. His defying his doctor's orders didn't surprise me at all. I figured that when he continued to scuba dive for another eleven years, Bert got the better end of the deal. I couldn't imagine him sitting around like a dried-up old zucchini, doing large-lettered crossword puzzles through trifocals and talking about his bowel movements. He was not about to endure hell so he could get into heaven. He lived life fully and died doing what he loved. He followed his passion to the very last moment. Good for him.

What I learned from Mr. Everit:

- I have to walk in my own shoes, never someone else's.
- The mark of a good teacher is the success of his students in his absence.
- Enjoy people you love as if it is the last time you will see them. It might be.

Other stuff he said:

- It's never too late to be what you might have been.
- To know what you prefer rather than simply saying "amen" to what the world tells that you should prefer, is to have kept your soul alive. (Robert Louis Stevenson)
- Your future isn't what it used to be.

What I did:

- Went to see my mom and told her how much I loved her.
- Made a list of what I would do if I had a year to live, and made plans to do it.
- Framed a photo of Bert Everit in his scuba gear, and put it on the edge of my desk.

A Will and a Way

A month later I received a phone call from Mr. Everit's attorney, Bob Kendall. He was a nice enough guy; I'd met him a few times. "Mr. Everit has named you in his will. Can you come to my office?"

I never expected that. But, then again, I never expected half the things he did.

As I drove downtown, I wondered what he could have possibly left me. He had already given me the keys to his kingdom, not to mention a whole new life. I really didn't want anything else from him, and I certainly didn't need it. I had enough money. And now enough belief.

Bob Kendall welcomed me to his office and invited me to sit on the plush chair in front of his desk. I looked around to see if anyone else from Mr. Everit's family was in the waiting room. They weren't. "Where is everyone else?" I asked.

"I held a separate reading for them. Be assured he has provided for them nicely. His will stipulated that I speak to you privately."

This was getting weirder by the moment.

The attorney took out a handwritten piece of paper and set it on the desk before him. He seemed nervous. "Bert cared about you very much," he stated in a sober yet kind voice.

"I know . . . he was like a father to me."

Bob looked me in the eye for a longer time than I was comfortable with. He cleared his throat and clutched the paper harder. Then he continued with a tiny clutch in his voice. "As you know, Mr. Everit held on for a few days in the hospital before he passed away. He wrote this in the presence of his wife and asked that his will be amended in accord with his wishes. Those wishes are stated in this document."

The lawyer took another deep breath and began to read.

To My Favorite Wheelbarrow Builder,

I was surprised he would start like that. Maybe he was a little woozy on painkillers.

I wish I could speak to you in person. I wanted to look you in the eye and tell you some things when I returned, but here I am in some dinky medieval hospital in the middle of nowhere, and God only knows if I will ever get out. Just in case I don't, I am sending you this letter. Please forgive me for not speaking to you face to face. I guess I made a mistake in assuming I would see you again. I once told you that life is like an answering machine, and you never know how long you'll have to leave your message, so say the important stuff first. I should have taken my own advice.

You once asked me if I made any mistakes, and I told you I had made one big one I was still trying to rectify. I hope this letter will finish the job.

Bob Kendall paused and looked up at me with tentative eyes. I nodded for him to continue.

In 1967 I was drafted to serve in the military. A year later I was dispatched to fight in Vietnam. Before I left, I married my high school sweetheart and we had a baby together. I am writing now to tell you that girl was your beautiful mother and that baby was you.

A jolt of energy shot through me. My gut clenched and I sat up ramrod straight. "No way!" I blurted out. "It can't be true!"

The lawyer pursed his lips and nodded. "I have known this for a while," he admitted. "Bert confided in me. I know it's hard to take . . . would you like some water, or want to get some air?"

I thought my head was going to explode. But I needed to hear the rest. "No . . . just keep going," I told him. I fell back in my chair, utterly shocked.

During a skirmish in a small village, I was captured and taken prisoner by the Viet Cong. They stuck me in a God-awful camp with meager rations, and every day I thought I would die the next. My only solace was to look up at the stars at night— the same stars you and I looked at together —and remember there was a bigger picture to life than the one in my face. In the midst of that hellhole I developed a powerful inner strength, a faith in good beyond appearances. It was the only way I could keep my sanity and survive. The man you met and knew was a result of the will I developed by struggling to keep my heart open in the darkest of conditions.

Why hadn't he told me? He could have told me. I would have understood.

When the war ended, the Viet Cong released me. But I was disoriented. They had tried to torture me into giving them military information, but I didn't. Yet their attempted brainwashing had affected my reasoning ability. I was too frightened to come back. I stayed in the jungles of Vietnam for another few years, trying to regain my clarity. Then I met a monk who taught me meditation and helped me find inner peace. That monk was the man you saw in the picture that fell out of my wallet. My hair and beard grew long while I hid in the jungle.

So that was it. I never really believed he was a hippie, anyway. The John Deere cap was a dead giveaway.

Finally I found the courage to come back to the states. I asked around until I learned where you and your mom lived. By that time you were maybe 10 years old. Your mom had given me up for dead, and remarried. I couldn't bear to mess up her life again. So I assumed another identity. I took an apartment near you and watched you grow up from afar. I was so proud to see you mature into a fine young man. But the longer time went on, the more terribly empty I felt being separated from you.

This all sounded too bizarre to be true. But he wouldn't make this up. My mind was racing out of control.

A year ago, I could no longer live with the distance between us. I was getting older, and the thought of living the rest of my life and dying without being close to you became unbearable. So I sent you a letter announcing the job opening here. I made it look like a form letter that went out to a lot of people, but it was only for you. You can imagine my joy when you came to the factory and we hit it off. When you accepted the job, I saw my opportunity to have a relationship with my long-lost son.

So many times I wanted to tell you all this, but I knew the kind of waves it would make. So I just enjoyed our being together; it was as if you had grown up with me your whole life, and now I was turning my business over to you. The day I did was the happiest day of my life.

I wanted to use my vacation time with Marlene to tell her all this. She was stunned, as I know you must be. But she loves me and she has grown to love you. She was happy I was going to tell you when we got back.

And now I am not sure if I will see you again. So I wanted to be certain you heard this from me rather than second-hand. In the event we do not meet again, please forgive me for not being the father I could have been. I hope that the time and connection we shared will somehow express to you how much I love you and believe in you.

With all my heart,

Your father,

Bert Everit

I tried to fight back the tears, but couldn't. Bert Everit, the kindest and most wonderful man I had ever met, was the father I never knew.

Bob Kendall finished reading and found my tear-laden eyes. I felt embarrassed, but I didn't really care. Bob understood.

"Anything else I need to know?" I asked. "Like, was he really Elvis?"

Bob smiled. "He left you two items." The attorney reached into his desk drawer and took out a small envelope and a thin square package hand-wrapped in brown paper. He gently pushed both items across the desk to me.

On the envelope I saw written in Bert's—my dad's—handwriting, *Somehow It All Works Out*. I opened it up. My God, it was his stock in the company. He owned more than half the shares. It took my breath away. This piece of paper meant I would never have to worry about money again. But then again, if I practiced what he had taught me, I never had to worry in the first place.

I stared at the package for a while. "I think I know what's in there," I told the lawyer.

Silently he gestured for me to open it.

I undid the wrapping and found a little note, also in my dad's handwriting.

All you ever need to know about running a wheelbarrow factory.

Inside I found Bert Everit's tattered copy of *Good Lemonade*.

Acknowledgments

I am deeply grateful to the following people for supporting me and Mr. Everit richly through love, skill, word, and deed to bring this story and its principles into manifestation:

Dee H. Winn, for her continual, constant, ever-empowering love, enthusiasm, and vision to find beauty, depth, and meaning in me and this book.

Michael Ebeling, for his astute business management skills and unconditional support to bring forth the highest creativity and deliver it to those who can benefit from it.

Ana Hays, for her administrative expertise, writing skills, and joyful attitude.

Pat MacEnulty, for her wise, heartfelt, and extremely helpful editorial insights.

Kristelle Sims Bach, for her eagle literate eye and talent to call *Mr. Everit's Secret* to highest potential.

Bob Friedman and the editorial and artistic staff at Hampton Roads, for their belief in *Mr. Everit* and their awesome abilities to bring forth the story in the most elegant and attractive format.

Bert Everit, wherever he is, for reminding me and all of us to wear our gold on the inside.

About the Author

Alan Cohen is the author of 20 popular inspirational books, including the best-selling *Why Your Life Sucks and What You Can Do About It*, the award-winning *A Deep Breath of Life*, and the classic *Are You as Happy as Your Dog?* He is a contributing writer for the New York Times #1 best-selling *Chicken Soup for the Soul* series. His books have been translated into 15 foreign languages.

Each month Alan's column, *From the Heart*, is published in many magazines and his interviews have been featured in numerous publications. He is a frequent guest on national radio and television and his presentations are regularly broadcast via satellite on the Wisdom Channel.

Alan is a faculty member at Omega Institute for Holistic Studies and is a popular keynote speaker for corporate, educational, and health conferences internationally. He also guides groups on excursions to sacred sites such as Machu Picchu, Bali, and Egypt.

Alan resides in Maui, Hawaii, where he conducts retreats in life mastery.

For information on Alan Cohen's books, tapes, online prosperity programs, Hawaii retreats, journeys to sacred sites, and seminars in your area:

Visit: www.alancohen.com
E-mail: info@alancohen.com
Phone: 800-568-3079 or 808-572-0001
Fax: 808-572-1023, or
Write to:
Insights for Richer Living
P.O. Box 835
Haiku, HI 96708

Personal Study with Mr. Everit

If you have found Mr. Everit's success principles inspiring, and would like to bring them to life in your career, finances, and relationships, you can deepen your experience through one or more of Alan Cohen's courses:

Relax into Wealth

- Rapidly shift your thoughts and attitude to allow more money, success, joy, and good into your life
- Receive an inspiring lesson per day via e-mail for 30 days, including fun and effective exercises to open your mind and get prosperity flowing
- Participate in a live teleseminar with Alan, during which you can ask questions and receive feedback to enhance your progress

The Year of Living Prosperously

- A dynamic one-year success course that will help you understand why and how prosperity works and will create significant changes in many aspects of your life

- Receive a dynamic lesson per week via e-mail for 52 weeks, with many valuable examples, exercises, and affirmations
- Participate in a monthly teleseminar with Alan, during which you can ask questions and receive feedback to enhance your progress

Life Mastery Training

- A six-day in-depth experiential course to get you in touch with your passion, purpose, and power, and help you make life decisions in harmony with your goals
- Held at a magnificent retreat center in Maui, Hawaii with a maximum of 30 participants
- Study directly with Alan and make the most progress in the shortest amount of time

For schedule and more information, visit

**www.alancohen.com,
e-mail info@alancohen.com, or
phone 800-568-3079**

Hampton Roads Publishing Company
. . . for the evolving human spirit

Hampton Roads Publishing Company
publishes books on a variety of subjects including
metaphysics, health, visionary fiction,
and other related topics.

For a copy of our latest catalog,
call toll-free, 800-766-8009,
or send your name and address to:

Hampton Roads Publishing Company, Inc.
1125 Stoney Ridge Road
Charlottesville, VA 22902
e-mail: hrpc@hrpub.com
www.hrpub.com